THAT FURTHER SHORE

Endorsements

Success isn't only about setting goals, it's about keeping on track. In *That Further Shore*, Sarah Arnot combines inspiring stories with useful tools to keep you productive and above all, to stay focused on your most important priorities.
Pieter Engelbrecht, CEO, Shoprite Holdings Ltd

We are always looking for ways to make our lives better. In *That Further Shore* Sarah Arnot does a fantastic job encapsulating in very concise and readable terms what we can do to improve our lives and achieve our goals. All of us can take something from this.
His Excellency Liam Mac Gabhann, Ambassador of Ireland, Embassy of Ireland, Pretoria

That Further Shore will resonate with anyone asking: "What next?" In *That Further Shore* book guides you into setting your compass and understanding how to reach your ambitions, whether you are young and setting out on your career journey, or a successful manager who wants to take the next step into corporate leadership.
Deborah Williams - Organisational Development Consultant, MMI

That Further Shore is a delightful guide full of important information for those of us who want to pursue our goals and enjoy life.
Andile Balula, Eventing SA level 3 course builder, Federation Equestre International 1* & 2* XC Course Designer

Today we live life on steroids: Too much work, too much information, too much stress and too many expectations. Most of us end up complying with our circumstances rather than choosing who, where and what we want to be. This easy-reading, personalised book cuts through the noise, and offers five easy steps to a new and better you. There is nothing to lose, so don't wait.

Andrew Woodburn, Managing Director,
Woodburn Mann Executive Search Africa

Working with Sarah Arnot as my coach took away the fear of going into unknown territory. Once the fear was gone, she gave me tools and practical steps to take, and each success gave me the motivation to take the next step. She helped me believe in myself, which gave me confidence in my business and rippled into my personal life as well. What's even more exciting is that now that I have achieved my dream, I'm going to apply the same lessons to aim for even bigger things. **That Further Shore** shares many of Sarah Arnot's stories and the process we used in our work together. My successful and growing business is the proof that it works!

Colette De Vreis, Founder, Pilates for Life

Sarah Arnot has written a practical guide on how to achieve our dreams – reaching that further shore. This book includes a practical and useful guide to achieve our objectives and ultimately transform our life!

Victor Kotze, CEO, Prosperis

In **That Further Shore**, Sarah Arnot shares stories from the many facets of her life - coaching, the corporate world and sport - to illustrate some of the most recent scientific thinking on decisions and choice, how we end up where we are, and what we can do about it. Full of practical suggestions, at the core of the book is a useful process to kickstart thinking about what you want and getting it too. Whether you are starting out in your corporate career, or are at your zenith and thinking, "what next?", this is a great book to read from cover to cover and then to keep on hand to dip into as you need it.

Francois Strydom, Executive, EOH Legal Services

I have witnessed first-hand Sarah Arnot's ability to influence, change, motivate and lead a diverse group of people from good to great. As an athlete, she embodies the word 'grit', which can be described as the great blend of passion and perseverance. Her book is not a dry academic body of work. She has skillfully made it an inspiring piece of literature - kept alive by the stories woven appropriately into the themes. This book is a must-read for anyone with a dream!

Phil Cunningham, Founder, Sunrise Productions

That Further Shore contains many real-life adventures from own coaching experience. To be given exposure to other CEOs' thinking via her coaching model and their fuel for success is enriching. This is a book I will be sharing with my leadership team.

Derek Patrick, CEO, The Design Company

As an academic coach, I find Sarah Arnot's practical five steps to be an essential ingredient towards the ultimate success of each client's graduation – reaching their own 'further shore'. I highly recommend this book to anyone who is on a journey of personal, professional, or vocational development. Sarah Arnot's powerful stories are truly inspiring and I intend to share her book with all those who cross my path.

Caroline Dale, Director, The Thesis Coach

Copyright © KR Publishing and Sarah Arnot

All reasonable steps have been taken to ensure that the contents of this book do not, directly or indirectly, infringe any existing copyright of any third person and, further, that all quotations or extracts taken from any other publication or work have been appropriately acknowledged and referenced. The publisher, editors and printers take no responsibility for any copyright infringement committed by an author of this work.

Copyright subsists in this work. No part of this work may be reproduced in any form or by any means without the written consent of the publisher or the author.

While the publisher, editors and printers have taken all reasonable steps to ensure the accuracy of the contents of this work, they take no responsibility for any loss or damage suffered by any person as a result of that person relying on the information contained in this work.

First published in 2018.

ISBN: 978-1-86922-759-3
eISBN: 978-1-86922-760-9 (ePDF)

Published by KR Publishing
P O Box 3954
Randburg
2125
Republic of South Africa

Tel: (011) 706-6009
Fax: (011) 706-1127
E-mail: orders@knowres.co.za
Website: www.kr.co.za

Printed and bound: HartWood Digital Printing, 243 Alexandra Avenue, Halfway House, Midrand
Typesetting, layout and design: Cia Joubert, cia@knowres.co.za
Cover design: Marlene de'Lorme, marlene@knowres.co.za
Photograph from: Oceanscapes, reproduced with the kind permission of Renate Aller
Editing & proofreading: Jennifer Renton, jenniferrenton@live.co.za
Project management: Cia Joubert, cia@knowres.co.za

THAT FURTHER SHORE

*Turn your dreams
into goals and
make them reality*

by

Sarah Arnot

kr
publishing

2018

From the chorus of *The Cure at Troy*

Human beings suffer,
They torture one another,
They get hurt and get hard.
No poem or play or song
Can fully right a wrong
Inflicted and endured.

The innocent in gaols
Beat on their bars together.
A hunger-striker's father
Stands in the graveyard dumb.
The police widow in veils
Faints at the funeral home.

History says, don't hope
On this side of the grave.
But then, once in a lifetime
The longed-for tidal wave
Of justice can rise up,
And hope and history rhyme.

So hope for a great sea-change
On the far side of revenge.
Believe that further shore
Is reachable from here.
Believe in miracle
And cures and healing wells.

Call miracle self-healing:
The utter, self-revealing
Double-take of feeling.
If there's fire on the mountain
Or lightning and storm
And a god speaks from the sky

That means someone is hearing
The outcry and the birth-cry
Of new life at its term.

Seamus Heaney

Table of Contents

Acknowledgements	iii
About the author	v
Preface	vi
Introduction	viii
Part I: That further shore	**1**
Chapter 1: The story of an entrepreneur	3
Chapter 2: Inspiration and motivation	11
Chapter 3: Choice and frames	17
Chapter 4: Process	21
Chapter 5: Focus	27
Chapter 6: Information	37
Chapter 7: Learning as adults	41
Chapter 8: People are different	47
Chapter 9: Humility	53
Part II: The 5-Step process	**57**
Chapter 10: Setting objectives	59
Chapter 11: Planning can change your life	65
Part III: Commitment	**91**
Chapter 12: Integrity	93
Chapter 13: Priorities	97
Chapter 14: Change and choice	109
Chapter 15: Self-management	119
Conclusion	**124**

Appendix I: Sources of information and learning   126
Appendix II: Summary of the 5-Step process   130
References   **135**

Table of Figures

Figure 1: Pilates for Life SWOT analysis   7

Figure 2: Pilates for Life buckets   8

Figure 3: Competency learning model   42

Figure 4: Kolb's learning cycle   44

Figure 5: Example of a dream sheet   76

Figure 6: Sarah's objectives   82

Figure 7: Breaking actions down and sorting them into buckets   87

Figure 8: Planning the year   88

Figure 9: The Eisenhower Matrix   100

Figure 10: The Eisenhower Matrix explained   101

Figure 11: The Eisenhower Matrix filled in from my To Do list   102

Acknowledgements

This approach to setting objectives has been around for a while. I've seen a version of it from James Clear, who has a blog well worth following: http://www.jamesclear.com.

I've seen and used another version from Kate Harrison, author of *The 5:2 diet*, which I've been following for years: http://kate- harrison.com/5-2diet.

Thank you to both of them for the inspiration to write this book.

I would like to express deep gratitude to my coaching clients, especially to those who have allowed me to share their stories in this book. Thank you also to the executive assessment clients I've worked with over the years and to my ex-colleagues at Spencer Stuart as well as my new colleagues at the Woodburn Mann Leadership Science Institute. Special recognition goes to the Western Cape Eventing Association council members – we had a lot of fun and a glorious nine years together. If I have something to say, it's thanks to all of you.

I'm incredibly lucky to have my brothers, Graham Mulhern and Mark Mulhern, and bless technology for enabling us to stay such close siblings and friends even though we live so far apart. You constantly challenge me to push harder and think further; I could not do it without you.

A book takes a huge amount of effort and input from an array of people. I would particularly like to thank the people who reviewed early or late versions of the text and offered critical feedback and support. Caroline Dale, Victor

Kotze and Deborah Williams, you are a remarkable trio of friends and your support and encouragement mean so much. My stepchildren, Robyn, Lauren, Christopher and Alistair (step-in-law), helped me edit the first edition of this book and gave me great comments and insights. How lucky I am that you became my family when I married Peter.

Thank you to Ilze Visage who created the beautiful illustrations in this book.

I first laid eyes on Sophie Kevany more than 40 years ago on my first day at Rathdown School; we were just nine years old. Our friendship has endured time and change and is precious beyond words. Sophie is a professional writer and journalist and helped edit this book. Any mistakes are mine, and were it not for Sophie's eagle eye, there would be many more.

Most of all I would like to thank my husband, Peter, who puts up with me spending hours in the office, studying or writing books, when we could be out having fun together. Your love means the world to me and I dedicate this book to you.

About the author

Sarah Arnot Mulhern is Managing Partner of the Woodburn Mann Leadership Science Institute, which provides leadership development and assessment services to Boards, CEOs and senior executives in South African corporate businesses.

Sarah's career spans more than 25 years, most of it spent at two companies - Accenture and Spencer Stuart - based in Ireland, France, the UK and South Africa. She held international leadership roles in both organisations. As an executive search consultant at Spencer Stuart she led the European Internet Practice and the European Software Practice. After moving to South Africa, she joined the Leadership Advisory Services (LAS) practice, consulting to global clients in multiple industries.

Sarah gives motivational talks based on her experience in sport and business, and offers expert leadership advice on television and radio.

Sarah is also an amateur three-day eventer, which is a three-phase Olympic equestrian sport that includes dressage, show jumping and cross country. She has held leadership roles in the sport, acting as President of Western Cape Eventing for nine years and sitting on the Board of Eventing SA.

Sarah holds BA (Hons) and MA degrees from Trinity College, Dublin and an MPhil (Executive Coaching) from the University of Stellenbosch Business School.

Preface

For almost 20 years my job has been to interview and assess senior executives all over the world because they were involved in an executive search process that I was running, because I had been asked to assess them for a leadership role, or as part of a corporate succession planning process. During those years, I observed that executives fell into one of two categories, neither of which had anything to do with culture, education or training; they either took control of their career path, or they let their career happen to them. Turning my attention to my friends and acquaintances I saw the same thing happening. No matter who they are, people often allow life to happen to them, responding to opportunities instead of deciding what they want out of life. I probably fell into the more passive category, until I came across this approach to choosing what you want and working out how to get it. There's nothing wrong with taking advantage of opportunities when they come up, but why wait? Why not create your own opportunities?

As I began to understand more about pro-active life planning, I decided to gather my client experiences into a book and combine it with academic research on leadership and human behaviour. This book is full of stories, research, ideas and inspiration, and offers a 5-Step process to help you apply those findings to your own life, changing it forever and for the better.

I understand that life can be hard. I've had my fair share of sadness, maybe more than my fair share, so I know how tough life can be from personal experience. Hope keeps me going when the tough times come; the hope that with time, and if we make the right choices, things will change. That is the theme of the chorus of Seamus Heaney's '*The Cure at Troy*'.

Believe that further shore may be reachable from here.

Your life. How to discover what you want.
Then make sure you get it.

Introduction

Do you know what you want out of life? Or even out of one year of your life: this year?

The aim of this book is to give you a way to identify what you really want out of life and to put a plan in place to deliver exactly that. How simple does that sound? It's quite a straightforward concept and if you want to get on with it, head on to Part Two to begin the 5-Step process. But before you go...

I published the first edition of this book, *Achieve Your Dreams*, in January 2017, and I collected feedback from my clients and friends on how useful they found the 5-Step process. I did not expect the response that I got. Every single person who followed the plan and wrote down their themes and objectives, achieved those objectives. Every single one. Even if they did not look at the plan again for the entire year, when they went back to it at the end of the year they found they had achieved their objectives and had even found them easy to achieve.

Even more people told me that they found it too hard to pin down their themes and objectives, so they gave up before they had finished the five steps. Because they did not set objectives, it was hard to tell what they had achieved.

All of which was great news. I cannot promise you that if you set out what you want as described in this book you will get it. No-one can promise you that, but there's strong evidence that if you do put some objectives down on paper and think about how you are going to achieve them, you'll do just that.

I picked three themes for myself last year - work, study and eventing. Eventing is an Olympic sport that involves three disciplines: dressage, cross country and show jumping. Training for all three is time-consuming.

One of my objectives was to qualify for the next level up and I did not achieve it. I feel quite good about it though, because I had clear priorities: first study, then work, then sport. I sacrificed quite a few competitions to put in enough study hours to complete my MPhil. Then my horse hurt himself, not seriously, but enough to miss the South African Championships. I do sport for fun and it cannot always have the priority I would like to give it. In the meantime, I nailed my other objectives. In fact, I wish I'd set even bigger objectives. More about that later.

Before you head off to the 5-Step process in Part Two, I would like to tell you about some of the challenges my clients have faced. There's a lot of research available on human behaviour and why we behave the way we do, but research is dry and can be dull to read. Stories are more interesting, so I've chosen some great ones that illustrate how certain behaviours can help or hinder us. When we challenge ourselves with goals, we have to figure out how we are going to change our behaviour in order to achieve those goals. These stories illustrate some of the changes my clients have made.

I cannot thank my clients enough for allowing me to talk about our work together. Some names have been changed and some are real. Sometimes the stories come from several clients, combined into one story for simplicity's sake.

You could see this book as a coaching conversation. In it you'll find ideas and stories from real coaching sessions, what happened and how clients' lives changed as a result.

Remember though, coaching doesn't change a client's life, clients do. A good coach is no more than a sounding board and a catalyst, helping the client explore their thinking and make better choices; choices that already exist, but that only become obvious as they take the time to think more deeply about their options.

Some of the stories are about leadership. Leadership theory applies to all of us because each of us is our own leader. That means that what you read about leadership applies directly to you and can help you achieve your goals. That is one of the themes of this book. Be your own leader, and above all, be true and honest with yourself.

The next theme is about setting some big goals. In the past I've recommended setting achievable goals, but my ongoing study of business and sports goal setting has changed my view. If the friends and clients who followed the 5-Step process last year achieved their objectives with ease, maybe they could have set bigger goals.

There are times when it's sensible to set SMART (Specific, Measurable, Achievable, Realistic and Timed) goals and there are times when you want to be ambitious and see if you can achieve the unthinkable. This year I'm going big and, if it's the right time for you, I encourage you to go big too.

> *If this is your year: Go Big.*

When you set your goal at 100, you achieve 100. When you set it at 1000 you might only achieve 500, but that is still five times more than 100.

The third theme might be the most important.

> If you want to achieve greater success, you are going to have to do things a bit differently, and that requires learning.

I've accrued many benefits from my years spent studying coaching and leadership. One of those is a far better understanding of adult learning. As adults, we learn differently from children. Some people like to think and model things in their own mind before they'll try something new. Others like to jump right in and learn as they go. It doesn't matter which type of learner you are, the important thing is: never stop learning.

The challenge is that learning requires humility.

In sport, people run up against this problem all the time. People might learn to ride a horse, maybe even get a good horse and win a few prizes. Then a really good trainer comes into town. All too often, instead of taking every word this coach says as a pearl of wisdom and applying it to what they do, the rider goes into the lesson thinking, "I'll show them how good I am". They seek praise instead of constructive criticism, possibly even resenting the constructive criticism when it does come. As an adult, it can be hard to be the student again. Adjusting that mindset to become a seeker of information and knowledge is the only path to growth and change, and it requires a degree of humility.

I spent a lot of time in the past year thinking about humility because I've realised it takes some confidence to be humble and sometimes I lack confidence. I know I'm not the only one who struggles with this. To be humble you have to accept that others are better than you; that they know more than you do. That is not always so easy, but it might be worth thinking about. With humility comes the appreciation that we can learn from others; indeed that we can learn something from everyone. Open your mind to learning, from books and online sources, as well as from all those around you.

In Part One of this book, you'll find stories and themes from the coaching and the people I met during last year. In Part Two, you'll find the 5-Step process that will set you on the road to achieving your dreams. If you are keen to get going and to make your plan for the year, then head along to Part Two and get started. You can come back to some of the stories and insights when you are done. Part Three talks through some tools and techniques that might help keep us all on track as we strive to achieve our dreams.

At the back of the book I've included an appendix that gives you the 5-Step process without the additional stories and information. When you come back to do your plan again, maybe at the end of the year, you might find it helpful to go straight to that appendix to remind yourself of the process and some of the key ideas.

> This is your book, and if you follow the 5-Step process, you will reach that further shore and achieve your dreams. Please let me know how it goes.

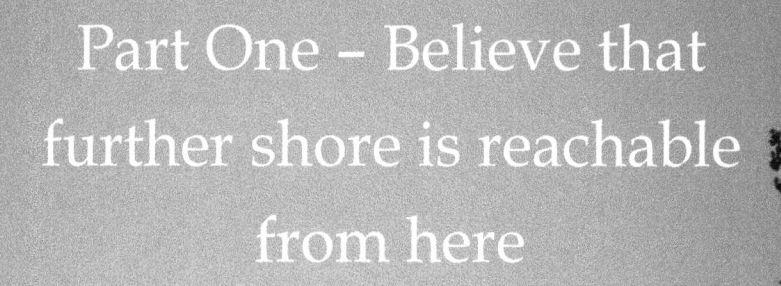

Part One – Believe that further shore is reachable from here

"If it doesn't challenge you, it won't change you."
Competeeveryday.com

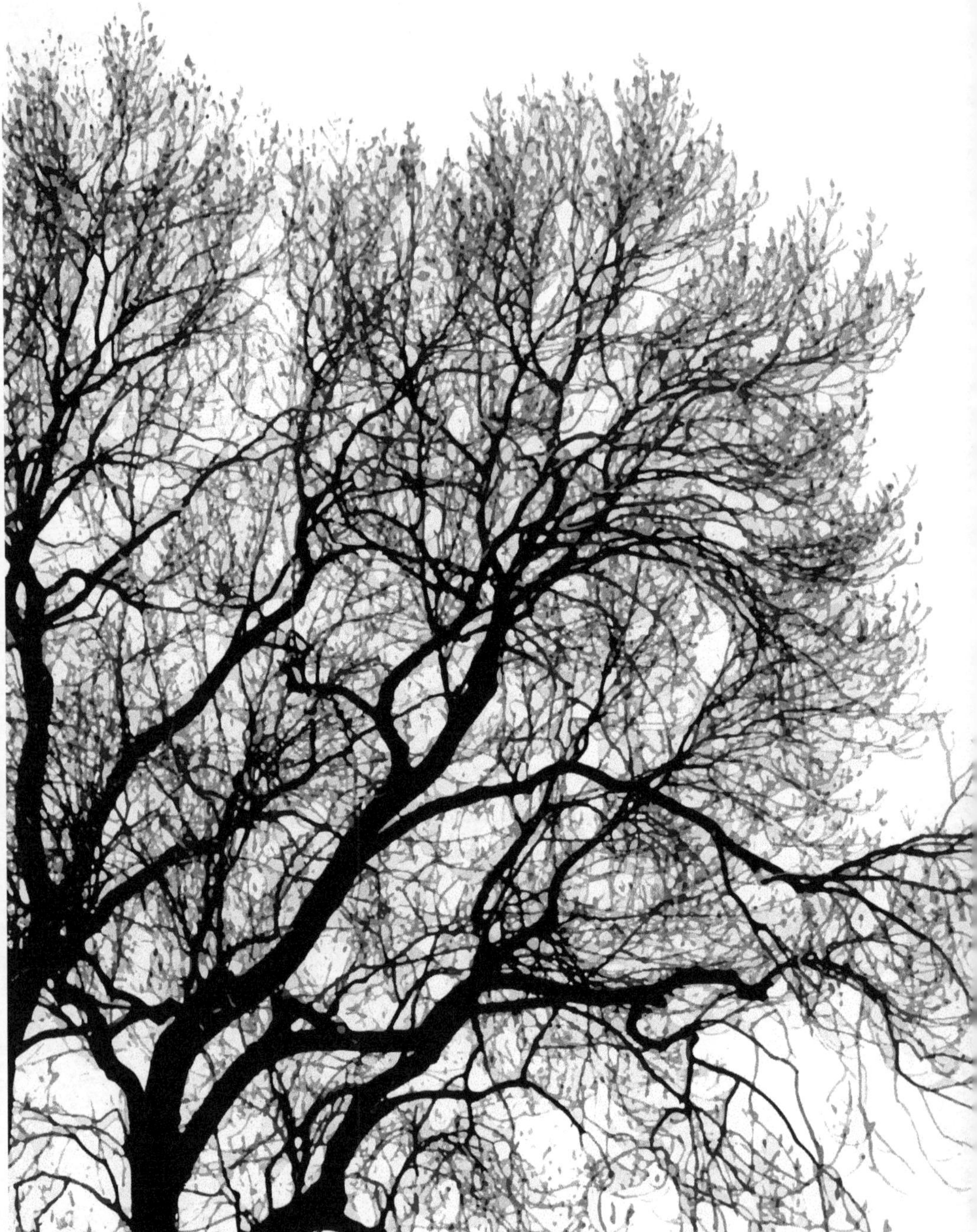

Chapter 1

The story of an entrepreneur

I met Colette after I'd broken my back falling off a horse. I always believed this was the worst thing that could happen to me in my riding career and when I hit the ground hard one day at a big show at the Riding Club in Noordhoek, a suburb of Cape Town, I immediately knew something was wrong. I stayed absolutely still. I remember thinking as I hit the ground, "This is a really bad fall". And the second thought was, "Wow, this is a really good hat", because I had smashed into the ground head first.

The paramedics skilfully loaded me onto a backboard that immobilised my spine and carted me off by ambulance to Constantiaberg Hospital. I will never forget the ER doctor coming up to me after looking at my x-rays and telling me I was fine. She said, "You have to learn to differentiate between muscle pain, rather than bone pain", as she pushed her finger hard into my C7 vertebra which we later found was broken in two places. "I'm pretty sure that is bone pain", I said, wincing. "No, you're fine, you can go home", she said dismissively, clearly thinking I was making a fuss about nothing.

By then, I'd been immobilised on a back board for about four hours with, as we later discovered, seven breaks in my vertebrae. Sitting up from that back board was the most painful thing I've ever done. It hurts even to think about it.

I spent most of the following week lying on a pile of pillows, working. If I did not move anything more than my fingers across the keyboard I was ok, but the minute I did I marvelled at the pain. On the sixth night, I was getting tingling down my arms and I thought, "This isn't right".

Peter, my husband, came home from an overseas trip the next morning and took me straight to our doctor. She said that I was probably fine, but loaded me up with serious painkillers and sent me to Dr Jack Eksteen, a spinal surgeon, to make sure.

Dr Eksteen immediately sent me off for an MRI, and when they saw the soft tissue damage on the MRI, he popped me into the CT scanner, which revealed the seven broken bones. Luckily it was the spinal processes that were broken, those little wings that stick out of each vertebra, so my spinal cord was not compromised and the fractures were stable. But it was just as well that I had not tripped and fallen during that first week and it certainly explained the pain.

I love South African doctors; they are completely different to the doctors I've met in other parts of the world. In Europe, doctors preach caution, but here in sports-mad South Africa, doctors, like everyone else, enjoy participating in sports, often extreme or dangerous ones like the ultra-marathon known as the Comrades race, or tough mountain bike races, like the Cape Epic.

Dr Eksteen is a particularly keen motor bike rider, so he completely understood that the first thing I wanted to do was to get back on a horse. Because my fractures were stable he chose not to operate, assuring me that if I put up with the pain and was patient, letting the bones heal on their own, I would have much better movement in my spine than if he fused the bones. "You're tough and stoic enough", he said to me, "you'll be fine".

Nine months later the bones finally healed and he gave me the green light to get back on a horse. He also told me I would need to do Pilates for the rest of my life to manage the ongoing consequences of the major spinal trauma. When nerves have been badly damaged the muscles spasm, but Pilates can help to lengthen and strengthen those muscles, reducing the spasms and the consequent pain.

Dr Eksteen sent me to Colette De Vries who runs Pilates For Life in my home town of Paarl, telling me that she would know exactly how to handle my injuries and get me back to competitive riding. He was so right. Colette not only got me back to competition level, she has helped me to become a far better and stronger rider. Without her, I doubt I would have achieved my equestrian dreams. She has also become one of my closest friends.

Colette combines many of the attributes necessary for business success. Firstly, she is 100% committed to lifelong learning. She qualified long ago and teaches Pilates to aspiring Pilates teachers as well as to her own clients.

She spends her weekends studying exercise and movement, and regularly attends courses to increase and refresh her knowledge. She has a small business and a limited budget, and until very recently she held her classes in a converted garage at her house in Paarl.

Colette has a warm personality and a delightful sense of humour, which means classes with her are fun as well as demanding and highly engaging. Having watched her teach students who are aspiring Pilates coaches, I've seen how she places the wellbeing of her clients first. She tells them that how they are feeling on any given day is of no importance to the people they teach. Their job is to turn up on time, indeed five minutes early, with a smile on their face and a heart open to the client's needs. As teachers, their focus must be outwards, not inwards.

So many of us working in business could benefit from this advice and over the years I've seen Colette put it into practice every day, no matter how she is feeling.

In 2016, Colette could not sleep at night. She has three children and she is a devoted wife and mother. Her middle son, Dante, is an exceptional rugby player who played on the legendary First team at his school, Paarl Boys High. In his final year, he was offered the chance to attend university in the UK and play rugby for the local team. Of course he wanted to do it, and Colette felt she could not hold her son back.

Three years of UK university fees is a lot of Pilates classes, particularly when those classes are in a weak and unstable currency like the South African Rand. At the same time, she felt that fear was holding her back and that she was slipping up on achieving her dream of building a really great Pilates studio, one that would help grow her business as well as motivate and inspire her clients to take greater care of themselves.

Colette and I sat down together and did some coaching sessions in 2016. Generally, I don't like to coach my friends, but I felt I could help her. Although my coaching is aimed at senior leaders in large corporates, I also thought it would be fun to coach an entrepreneur who had ambitions to change her world.

At the heart of coaching lies the client's need to tell their story to someone who is really listening, and in telling that story they must make sense of it to themselves.

Chapter 1: The story of an entrepreneur

As Colette told me her story it was obvious to both of us that there were plenty of actions she could take that would start a process of change in her business.

We used some tools to help her generate ideas, including a simple SWOT (strengths, weaknesses, opportunities and threats) analysis, which helped identify where she was positive, where her fears lay, and some ideas for solving problems.

Strengths	Weaknesses
o Solid client base	o Spending too much time on admin tasks
o Beginning of a good team in place	o Not marketing the business enough
o Ability to bring in and train more staff	o Too dependent on me as the trainer, need to develop the profile and client base of the other trainers
o Trusted by medical professional – a source of new clients	o Working from own home – means the family sometimes feel invaded
o Hardworking and ambitious	o No funds to finance expansion
o Great personality for this kind of work	o Hard to find the right location
o Excellent technical skills	o Feeling under financial pressure which could limit ability to act and grow
o Willing to continue investing and training	
o Amazing existing clients, which is why I love doing this	

Opportunities	Threats
o Influx of higher earning middle class clients to the local area – estates such as Val de Vie and Pearl Valley as well as Paarl itself	o Ex-students setting up competing studios (not a serious threat)
	o Inability to invest enough in the new studio
o Development in the town may lead to a suitable location	o Haven't found the right property
	o Expanding feels risky, fear is paralysing
o Could expand the team and teach them how to bring in new clients as well as training them in teaching pilates	o Not setting sights high enough
	o Finding the time to look for premises and set up new studios as well as teaching to bring income in
o More studios can generate more income	o Find the right people for the long term team
o Don't wait to find the perfect place, start growing the business and finding the right people now	o Not spending enough time marketing people seem to think we are "full"

Figure 1: Pilates for Life SWOT analysis

I also encouraged her to think about her business in a structured way. We created buckets that included HR, admin, sales and marketing, property, etc., and sorted the output of the SWOT analysis and other ideas into those buckets.

PILATES FOR LIFE

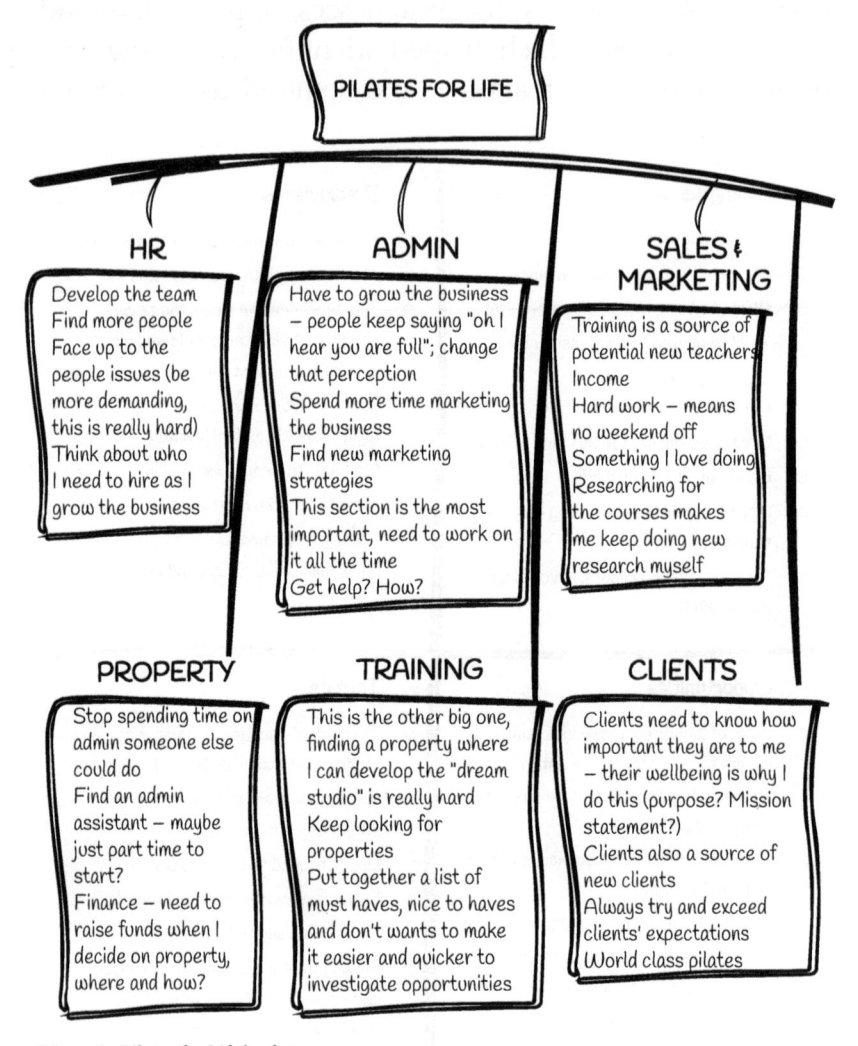

HR
- Develop the team
- Find more people
- Face up to the people issues (be more demanding, this is really hard)
- Think about who I need to hire as I grow the business

ADMIN
- Have to grow the business – people keep saying "oh I hear you are full"; change that perception
- Spend more time marketing the business
- Find new marketing strategies
- This section is the most important, need to work on it all the time
- Get help? How?

SALES & MARKETING
- Training is a source of potential new teachers
- Income
- Hard work – means no weekend off
- Something I love doing
- Researching for the courses makes me keep doing new research myself

PROPERTY
- Stop spending time on admin someone else could do
- Find an admin assistant – maybe just part time to start?
- Finance – need to raise funds when I decide on property, where and how?

TRAINING
- This is the other big one, finding a property where I can develop the "dream studio" is really hard
- Keep looking for properties
- Put together a list of must haves, nice to haves and don't wants to make it easier and quicker to investigate opportunities

CLIENTS
- Clients need to know how important they are to me – their wellbeing is why I do this (purpose? Mission statement?)
- Clients also a source of new clients
- Always try and exceed clients' expectations
- World class pilates

Figure 2: Pilates for Life buckets

It did not matter that at that stage there was only one person in HR and no-one in admin; the idea was to put some shape and structure around the business. Actions quickly emerged from that exercise that enabled Colette to think in a more structured way about how to move forward. For example, she did not have any administrative assistance, so she was spending time on tasks that were not helping to grow the business in any way. She quickly found someone to help with administration in return for Pilates training.

Eighteen months later, having grown the business considerably, Colette partnered with the owner of Spice Route wine farm on the outskirts of Paarl, and in 2018 she finally opened her dream studio.

The location is stunning and will attract new clients. She will get her home back for the family. She will be able to grow the business as never before with three fully equipped studios offering a range of classes. She will also be able to grow her Pilates teacher training practice, already popular because of her unique style and her huge knowledge base. Her son went to university in Leeds and played rugby for the local team. He graduates in 2018 with an excellent degree in business studies.

The point of telling you this story is not to tell you that coaching helped Colette, although she gives our coaching sessions a lot of credit for where she is today. The point is that the only thing stopping Colette from achieving her dream was fear of taking action. In her case, taking action meant analysing her situation to understand what was important and what she could do to get started. And then to get on and do it. Not everything worked straight away. For example, she explored several different venues before finding the right one. But because she had sorted her actions into categories, or buckets, she was able to see that she was making progress in some areas while others took longer.

That progress motivated her to keep going with the bigger picture in mind.

Chapter 2

Inspiration and motivation

The power of small wins by Teresa M. Amabile and Steven J. Kramer was published in the *Harvard Business Review*, a publication I often mine for articles on leadership because they are based on academic research and then published in business language which makes them easier to read.

When Amabile and Kramer studied motivation, they found, somewhat to their surprise, that although people are motivated by power and money, what motivates us most of all is a feeling of progress, or what the authors call "small wins".

That is why it makes sense to break your ambitions down into smaller objectives and to break out the component pieces, like we did with Colette's business.

> If you feel you are making progress in some areas, it will help motivate you to keep going in others, which might be tougher and require persistence to achieve a breakthrough.

Another article talks about persistence being the main factor that leads to success, particularly for entrepreneurs. Most businesses don't fail because they weren't good ideas - they fail because people gave up too soon. I love the story of James Dyson, who went through hundreds, if not thousands, of iterations before he perfected his eponymous vacuum cleaner and changed vacuuming forever. Constant innovation and persistence led him to succeed. Along the way Dyson almost certainly had small wins that helped him to persist.

I recently listened to Arnold Schwarzenegger's autobiography, *Total Recall*. Anyone who knows me would be quite surprised to find me reading/listening to the action hero body builder's autobiography, so here is how it came about. I was reading *Tools of Titans*, a rather hefty book by Tim Ferriss that is packed full of great ideas and wonderful insights. *Tools of Titans* summarises the best content from the many leaders and thinkers that Ferris has interviewed over the years for his podcast. One of the interviews was with Schwarzenegger and I looked at it because at the back of my mind I always wondered how on earth Mr Universe from Austria came to marry a Kennedy, become a huge star and then Governor of California. The interview in *Tools of Titans* surprised me, not least because Schwarzenegger came across as playful, intelligent and very hard working. When I saw he'd written his autobiography my curiosity was piqued, so I listened to the audiobook and loved it. Schwarzenegger is energetic, thoughtful, humorous, open-minded and clear on his own ideas. He's also flawed, as all the best people are, and he's quite private, so I'm sure that there's a lot that did not make it into the book. He has a great memory and goes into detail about the early part of his career, when a lot of his learning about life took place.

One of the first things in the book to strike me was something he said about body building. He said, "My body really responded". This means he gained small wins all the time, which encouraged him to keep going and to be persistent over many years with weight-lifting repetitions in his quest to attain a form of physical perfection.

Another thing that struck me about this story is that it explains why I find the actual act of exercising so profoundly unrewarding. Since my early 20s I've run about 4km about three times a week, sometimes more, sometimes less. Occasionally I do a longer run, up to 10km. I will never run further than that; my body simply doesn't respond to all this exercise. For years I pushed harder by doing interval training and I even ended up with athlete's heart syndrome, which was diagnosed when my resting heart rate dropped to the low 40s and became irregular and quite uncomfortable. This is frankly ridiculous when you only run 40 minutes three times a week, even if you are doing interval training. My doctor thought it was very funny. I did not, and it did not go away until I broke my neck, which prevented me running for several months, and during that time my heart settled down. I went back to running as soon as I could, though I dropped the interval training and I don't push myself to the max any more. I run for many reasons. It doesn't help me to lose weight, but I suspect it may help prevent me gaining weight, and I've joked that I run away from the fat person I don't want to be. I do some of my best thinking while I'm out running. When I travelled a lot, having a pair of running shoes meant I could always exercise, in a hotel gym if I had to. But my body just doesn't respond. There's no satisfaction. Yet despite the lack of reward, I've been hauling myself out there three times a week for the last 25 years. What is motivating me? What are the small wins that keep me going through the seasons and the years, and, hopefully, many years to come?

The answer is partly keeping the fat away, partly to enjoy what I see around me and be outside, and partly because the post run euphoria is terrific. I always try to run first thing in the morning, when my motivation is highest. And cities are more interesting at that time of day, before the general populace is on the move. The farm where I live is beautiful at dawn. So is my home town, in County Wicklow in Ireland. Then there's the thinking – the free ranging of the mind in a state of what Mihaly Csikszentmihalyi called "flow". Just being out in the air, not thinking about anything in particular and letting the body move freely, liberates my mind to range across any number of topics and come up with new ideas. Where else do you spend 40 minutes with no distractions, no messages, no email, no Facebook, not driving, or talking, or sitting in a meeting? Not thinking about what you need to do, or rushing through to the next item? There's nothing but putting one foot in front of the other in the morning air. That is also a "win". No matter how hard it is to keep putting one foot in front of the other, I never regret it once I'm out there. I know I can survive the 40 minutes and that too sustains motivation; it helps me to persist at running week in, week out. Year in, year out.

> You do not always have to chase a big goal; sometimes it's the small commitment, like the running, that keeps us in good health over the years and gives us the consistent small wins that can sustain motivation over extended periods of time.

Whether your goals are large or small I encourage you to apply the 5-Step process in Part Two, to figure out your themes and objectives. Then you can plan how to achieve them by breaking each objective into small, manageable steps to get you started.

Chapter 2: Inspiration and motivation

You can use the same planning process with colleagues at work - all it takes is a flip chart or a big white board and a brainstorming session. But beware. I've found that teams come up with a whole bunch of great ideas, but then they find it really hard to whittle it down to just 3-5 themes for the year. They want to do it all. The reality is, if you have too many themes you might not achieve any of them, so you need to focus on the most important, exactly as you need to do in your own life. You can keep the rest as back-up, so that if you unexpectedly deliver early, you can add to the list.

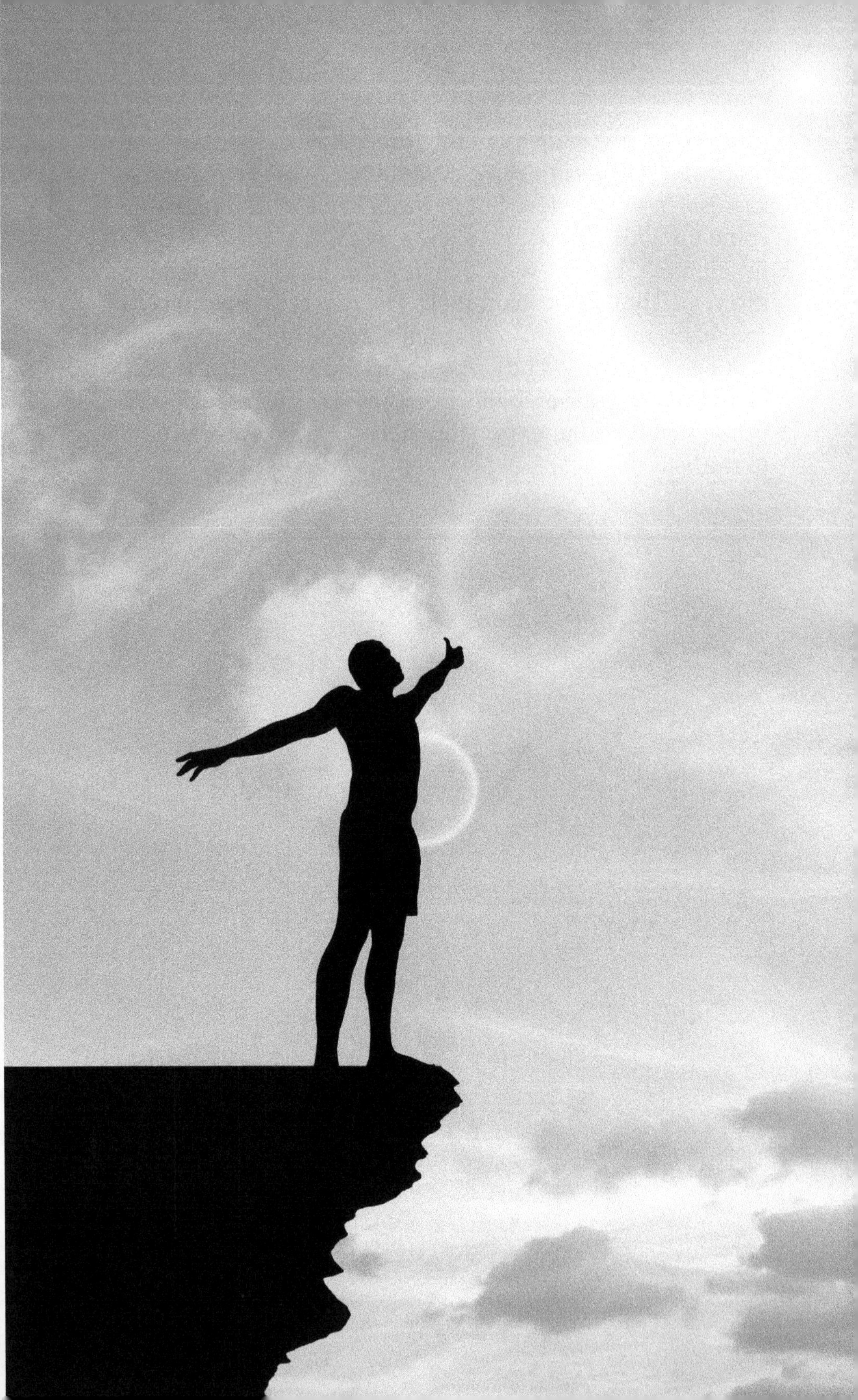

Chapter 3

Choices and frames

Sometimes you'll accidently restrict yourself because you unconsciously limit your choices. This is something coaches see a lot and it's also one aspect of behavioural economics that plays into coaching, a point I'll explain after I've told you about Jerome, who works for a major insurance firm.

Jerome was identified early on by his boss as someone who takes ownership, gets the job done and delivers. Whenever his boss changed jobs, he made sure to bring Jerome along with him, which has led to some interesting career development opportunities.

Yet Jerome reached a stage where he felt stuck. He had grown and changed into a more mature and competent leader, but his boss was still seeing the same person he had always seen. This meant that Jerome did not always receive the credit and opportunities he deserved.

Jerome was so frustrated that he was thinking of leaving the business. "Before you do that Jerome", I said, "let's just talk about the situation here and whether you have the power to change some of the things you do not like. Rather than move away to another company, which might be no better, why don't we identify what you really want and see if you can get it here, where you are now?" The company is one with a good reputation for treating employees well, particularly in terms of training and career development, so I genuinely felt that Jerome should explore all his options before taking a decision that might not benefit him in the long term.

We talked about the challenge and I asked him, "Who is responsible for your career development?" "My boss", was the reply. "Really?" I asked. "Yes, but nothing is happening." So I asked, "What can you do about that?" Jerome paused and thought for a long moment. "I suppose I could take the responsibility myself?" My next question was, "If you did, if you had the freedom to do that, what kind of choices would you make?" Enthusiasm began to sound in Jerome's voice. "I could make a plan of what I wanted, and then start working towards that." "Would it change your relationship with your boss?" I asked. Another long pause. "You know, I think it would", said Jerome. "I wouldn't feel I depended on him so much. In fact, it might make me feel like I owned the relationship and I could start managing the relationship and taking responsibility for it." His face lit up as he thought about it.

Our next session was about a month later and the man who walked into our meeting room was a completely different person. His face was alive and before I could say a word he said:

"Sarah, I have to tell you, this has been the most amazing month of my life. After our meeting, I suddenly realized that I own my job, and what I do, and that I can change the relationships around me if I want to. I went to my boss with a plan. I didn't ask his permission, I just calmly told him what I was going to do, with the team, and for my own development. When he didn't give it his full attention, I called him on that and told him that he needed to take his management role more seriously. At first he was surprised, but then he responded really well. He started looking at me differently and from then on, he saw me differently. Even in meetings he's been treating me with respect and he steps back when I speak up. I cannot believe how easy it was to change things and how much better I feel. I've been looking forward to this session so much so that I can tell you all about it."

Jerome continued in this vein for the rest of our session. From that moment on our coaching sessions were about using me as a sounding board for his ideas. Any thoughts of his leaving the business evaporated.

Jerome had found himself in a position where he did not believe he had the power to change things. He was frustrated and unhappy and thought his only choice lay in the status quo or leaving the company.

That kind of overly narrow framing of situations is a key topic in Daniel Kahneman's brilliant book, *Thinking Fast and Slow*. He shows how easily we fall into the trap of thinking that our choices are binary; that we have to choose between two options. If we broaden our frames and look at things differently, many more choices start to emerge.

Having a coach who listens with undivided attention and asks good questions can help clients to broaden their frames. The questions I asked Jerome were not particularly earth-shattering or sophisticated, but they helped him to think differently about his situation. Note the wording there… the coaching did not change Jerome's world, it was merely the catalyst that helped him change his own world.

> Simple as it may seem, the personal brainstorming in the 5-Step process can also help you to broaden your frames.

I love to bounce ideas off others, but sometimes that's not possible. When it's not, I apply step three of the 5-Step process. I make myself sit down with a sheet of paper and spend five or ten minutes writing down everything I can think of about the question at hand, with a focus on positive outcomes. It's like a mini, self-driven coaching session. I'm not particularly creative but I'm often amazed at what my mind comes up with when I force it to concentrate hard on something specific for a short period of time.

As you come up with more options and a greater range of choices using the 5-Step process, you may end up setting objectives or prioritising unexpected themes. There's nothing wrong with that; on the contrary, if that happens you should be proud of your work. It means you've identified new choices and potential for a greater range of possibilities.

In this chapter I've focused on encouraging you to use the brainstorming process in Step 3 to broaden your frames and help you to become aware of your full range of choices. There's another important aspect to choices, which is about the decisions we make every single day that either bring us closer to our goals or frustrate us by taking us further away. We're going to take a closer look at that when we get to Part Three.

Chapter 4

Process

Having a plan is a big part of achieving your goals. This book will help you figure out what actions you need to take for your plan to become reality. That is part of the process: anything you want to do well will involve a process of some kind.

The trouble is that perfecting a process is often boring, or just hard work. In sport, it's the hours and hours of practice that you put in; the training and the fine tuning and the constant challenging of your limits. In business, it's constantly improving your skills. As a leader that might mean intense periods of training, reading on the subject of management and leadership, improving your financial skills, or constant operational improvements.

If you have never done it before, you might want to invest in presentation skills - not only how to stand up and present, but also how to create great presentations and to put your message across powerfully.

There's so much available through the internet that can help you improve your processes, yet because it's the boring bit, we don't always do that. But remember this, when the chips are down, the person or the business with the best processes wins, and you want to be that person.

There's a great piece about this in James Kerr's *Legacy*, which is the story of how the All Blacks transformed a weak team in the mid-2000s into the winning machine they are now. The All Black's team management decided that they would consider every single process involved in delivering a world-beating game of rugby on the field and look for ways to improve each one. They figured that it might be very hard to improve a single process by 10%, but if you could identify a 1% improvement across many processes, you might end up with 10% improvement or even much more.

Schwarzenegger talks about process in *Total Recall* and I like what he has to say. What is relevant is his commitment to repetitions: what he calls reps. He learned early on, as he started building that famous body, that it's the commitment to the reps that gets the result - winning Mr Universe. He would make a plan for a long training session, decide what he wanted to do and chalk up lines on the wall in the gym in the small town where he lived in Austria. When he finished each series of reps he would put a cross through the line, until all the lines, maybe 50 or 60 in a session, were crossed off. Later, as Governor of California, a state far bigger than many small countries, he would still be there with his list of commitments, crossing them off one by one. As an action hero in films he does his own stunts because they can never find a body double who looks like him. To learn the hard stunts, he would do the reps. Say a scene required him to ride a motor bike backwards, shooting at his opponent. He would practice handling the gun, then riding the bike, then turning around and riding the bike backwards, then riding the bike backwards handling the gun. On and on until it was just right, so that when the cameras rolled the stunt was a single, perfect take.

Breaking something down into its component parts and then building it up again until you've got it right is central to achieving your goals. This doesn't just apply to sport. For example, self-management is an important part of leadership. Applying process to self-management involves researching it, understanding the component parts and then "doing the reps". In the case of self-management that might mean responding calmly and consistently even when other people get heated. Or committing only to those things you really will deliver. In that case, doing the reps is about delivering every time, so that it becomes a smooth consistent routine that your colleagues can rely on.

On its own, process is not enough; you need to improve and refine it all the time. Schwarzenegger became particularly adept at looking at his own body from a neutral perspective, identifying weaknesses and then adjusting his training programme to address them. Most of us need to identify the process and then push ourselves out of our comfort zone, where we might make mistakes or even scare ourselves, but that is how we learn new things and refine our process.

We also need feedback from others - not just any others, but what Ray Dalio in *Principles* described as "credible others". In other words, people who are knowledgeable and expert in the field and who will give you honest and reliable feedback. Dalio is the founder of Bridgewater, one of the most successful investment firms in the world. Dalio's notion of "credible others" appeals to me because you need to separate expert opinion from the rest. That way, you will not only be able to identify the useful information and the best sources, but you will also benefit from the expert feedback loop, which, research has shown, gets us closer to achieving excellence.

One can apply this principle of continuous process improvement to many aspects of life, but it's not always easy. I find the hardest step of the 5-Step process is the final one, which is building your plan to achieve your goal. Thinking about the process that you need to put in place, as well as the reps that you need to do, can really help. When you set out to achieve something it can be exciting and motivating, and when you succeed the feeling of achievement is wonderful. Often there's a long stretch of time between those two where you plod away, working at your process, improving it and following it, and it may seem that not much is happening. The nature of change is that it's not always linear. We sometimes plateau for a while and then suddenly make a big jump forward. That is why it's so important to note and record those small wins. It's also why you need to look back from time to time so that you can see the progress you have made. All too often we see only the mountains we have still to climb and we forget how far along the road we have travelled.

One of my closest friends is the journalist Sophie Kevany. We have been friends since the age of nine when we found ourselves in the same class in school. She helped me with the editing of this book and on reading this section she reminded me of the days when we were still schoolgirls and she and her father used to go walking in the Wicklow mountains on Saturdays. They would walk for four or five hours at a time in all weathers. On a fine day Ireland is one of the loveliest places on earth and the Wicklow mountains one of the loveliest parts of the country. The problem with Ireland is that a fine day is a rare day. Walking in the howling wind, with the misty rain coming down sideways into their faces, John would stop a moment and get Sophie to turn and look behind. "Before we climb the next peak", he would say, "just take a moment to look at how far we have come". Sophie, all of 16 years old, would look back, note just how far they had come along the peaks and valleys of these granite-topped hills, then straighten her back and prepare to march forward.

> Support yourself on the journey by taking the time to think about how far you have come.

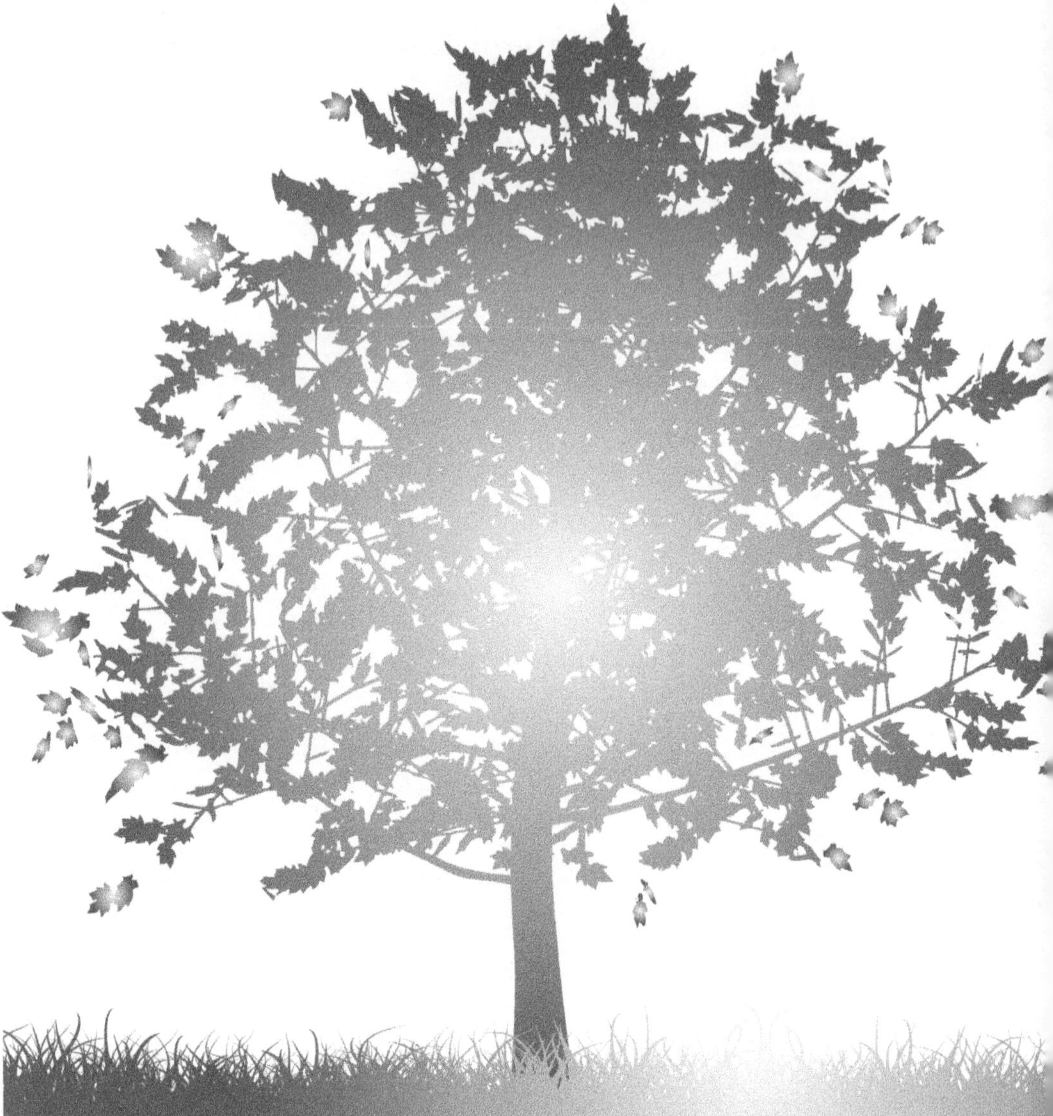

Chapter 5

Focus

My new business partner is Andrew Woodburn, Managing Partner of South Africa's leading boutique executive search firm. Woodburn Mann competes in the African market with big executive search firms (popularly known as "headhunters") like Spencer Stuart and Heidrick and Struggles. We have set up a new business, the Woodburn Mann Leadership Science Institute, to offer a range of leadership assessment and coaching services to CEOs and Boards on the African continent.

In the process of discussing how we will work together, I've come to know Andrew quite well. He is a high energy, intense individual who talks a lot. I don't know if I could have partnered with him a few years ago because I used to talk a lot too. Older now, and possibly a little wiser, I suspect that Andrew's intensity is his way of processing facts and situations, and that he needs that talking space in order to think. I'm comfortable to give it to him.

When Andrew meets someone, he zooms in on exactly what he needs from them. I mean that in a positive way – people come to headhunters for a purpose; they need to find a great executive or they want to talk about a job opportunity that has come up. They expect the headhunter's full attention. It's incredible to watch Andrew do this with a possible candidate. As he talks to them, his mind is picking up on everything they say and do, putting those pieces together with what he already knows about that person, what is on their CV, what the research team has said about them, and what any third parties have told him. When the executive leaves the room and you ask Andrew what he thought, he will give a concise summary of exactly why they will fit a role, or not. In listening to him, a neutral person in the room who had never been involved in search would ask, "How did you get all that information, and draw those conclusions?"

Like all great headhunters, Andrew does it because over the years his mind has become ever more attuned to what lies behind the responses given by each and every candidate. This is true expertise, which takes time to develop and refine. It is the businessperson's version of the 10,000 hours, in the context of executive search. You have probably heard of Malcolm Gladwell's idea that to achieve excellence in any field of endeavour, you must put in at least 10,000 hours of practice. I've chosen an example from my own world, that of leadership advisory and executive search, to show how experience and knowledge combine to enhance focus and allow seamless rapid processing. I suspect that all great leaders probably do this, consciously and unconsciously, joining the dots to form a comprehensive picture.

Pieter Engelbrecht, CEO of Shoprite Holdings, one of South Africa's largest companies, used an image that has stuck in my mind ever since he first described it to me. He said that shortly after he stepped into the CEO role, someone asked him what was it like. "There's no way to reply", he told me.

> *It's like when you walk into a room you've never been in before, your mind instantly processes all the data, the floor colouring, the size of the windows, the red chair in the corner, the type of lighting, the flowers, the people in the room. If you tried to describe it all it would take an age but your mind takes it in in an instant. This job is the same; there is so much information and data to process and my mind just does it at great speed.*

The years of senior leadership that led up to his appointment as CEO have enabled Pieter to process constantly at this speed, taking everything in, joining the dots, and keeping his focus on what is important.

This ability is described by Daniel Goleman, one of the most respected writers on leadership and excellence. He coined the term *'Emotional Intelligence'* in his book of the same name. A few years later he wrote another fundamentally important work, *Social Intelligence*. In 2013, Goleman turned his attention to *Focus, the hidden driver of excellence*.

Focus takes the concept of the 10,000 hours of practice a step further by suggesting that to become an expert, you have to focus on the right things; you must direct your attention, decide what you want, and then use a laser-like focus to achieve it. That is what Andrew Woodburn does - almost without thinking about it his mind filters the information he hears, like a brilliant tennis player lining up a great shot without allowing conscious thought to interrupt the process. He has trained his mind to focus on what it is about this person that will make them a perfect fit for a particular role.

In *Outliers*, Malcom Gladwell coined the phrase "the 10,000 hours" to describe the investment needed to achieve mastery in any field, but it was Geoff Colvin who took that a step further in his book, *Talent is Overrated*, published the same year. It is not that you need 10,000 hours of practice, he said, it's that your practice needs to be deliberate, disciplined and well designed in order to focus on the areas that need improvement. Goleman built on this when he wrote about focus, pointing out that the mind literally trains itself to notice what we focus on, so the improvements become hard wired in our brains.

If that sounds like hard work, you're right, it is. But learning and growing are among the most rewarding of human accomplishments, particularly when we stretch ourselves. No matter what you want to achieve, growing your knowledge and becoming an expert is one of the keys to success. The more you know at a great level of detail, the better you will be able to hone your mind and focus on what really matters.

Different tasks require different kinds of focus. When I started my academic research at the beginning of 2017 I was a complete novice, and as I read through the work of previous students, I had absolutely no idea how I could possibly accomplish a finished thesis.

Determined to succeed, I did some research on thesis writing, created a plan and committed to it with absolute focus. I love reading books about mountain climbing and equated it to the effort required to summit a Himalayan peak. I estimated the number of hours I thought it would take on a monthly basis and then made sure I did those hours. When I felt fresh and confident, I did the writing. If I did not feel like writing, I would read, find new articles, or research where I might find the articles that I needed. In research, there are always plenty of tasks that need to be done beyond the actual writing, because a requirement of academic writing is to show how the work was done and why the student took each of the various decisions involved. My commitment to the process ensured that despite some unexpected disruptions, I got to the end and submitted on time.

I've since shared this concept of focus with my clients and some of them have really benefitted. Melinda (not her real name) is a good example of how changing your focus can help bring about transformation in leadership. She was moving to a new job and was really excited about the possibility of a fresh start. She is a communications expert, hard-working and highly skilled, but she was not always good at building the quality relationships around her that she needs in order to be successful.

When she moved into her new job we discussed how she might focus a little less on the importance of the technical aspects of the job – as a genuine and experienced expert she could accomplish that with less effort – and much more on building relationships with her stakeholders from the start. That involved some of the skills that Goleman described in *Social Intelligence*, i.e. thinking about other people's motivations, putting herself in their shoes, and taking responsibility not only for the message, but also for how it lands and how it influences the behaviour of others.

Getting Melinda to shift her focus immediately helped her to build better relationships. Where she previously thought that the need to manage her stakeholders was something that got in the way of her work, she now sees it as a critical aspect of her job.

> Understanding what to focus on as your career grows is part of the challenge.

In Melinda's case, the first 15 years of her career involved building the technical expertise that means she is one of the most trusted communications experts in her world. Her success led to her being assigned a leadership role where she needed to delegate and deliver through others and to engage more broadly with peers, which she initially struggled with. Bringing that aspect of leadership to her attention, changing her focus, immediately helped her.

In my career as an executive search consultant, and in executive assessments, I've seen this happen many times. We build our careers, like Melinda did, by developing valuable skills and knowledge, which we develop as our careers progress. For many people this is enough to get them to a middle, or even senior, management position by their late 30s or early 40s. Stepping up to the next level requires new skills – most often the social intelligence skills that are sometimes referred to as "people skills". This is principally because the range of stakeholders with whom you need to engage has broadened considerably. Your relationship with your peers matters more at this level because you need to get things done as a team of equals, not just by yourself, and through those who report to you. The people who report to you also become more senior, with strong ideas and opinions of their own. Instead of telling them what to do, you need to understand how to motivate and inspire them.

Because we are social beings, understanding social intelligence is a first step to being successful in many aspects of life. Social intelligence is not about being popular and easy going, though those attributes may help. You don't need to be an extrovert to have high social intelligence; in fact, I've observed that extroverts can be lower in social intelligence than introverts, though I've not yet seen a study that backs that up. Social intelligence is about your ability to read other people and then to flex your own style to get the best out of any communications with them. As I described above when talking about Melinda, developing sophisticated social intelligence skills also means considering how your message will land with the other person and impact their behaviour in the future.

A broad focus can be a good thing

Does this mean you have to zone in on things and focus on one thing at a time? Not necessarily. Some people are successful because they can manage a lot of different moving parts at once. I'm not talking about multi-tasking, which has been proven not to exist; it turns out that not even women can really multi-task. There are, however, different kinds of intelligence, and we can improve our intelligence because we know our brain can be trained and grow. Think about this: world class CEOs and world class university professors are both extremely clever groups of people. The difference is that the CEO is broad, while the professor is deep. The way they focus is completely different: the CEO has to deal with constant change and complexity. They have to manage stakeholders, think strategically about the future and recruit a team of stars, while delivering immediate results. The professor will build a reputation on becoming an expert on one thing, often in a way that is difficult for the rest of the world to understand. When my stepson, Christopher, submitted his PhD thesis in biotechnology to the University of Cambridge, I thought I should read it, even if I did not understand much. I did not understand a single sentence. My respect for Christopher grew exponentially. He had undertaken an in-depth study of a highly technical topic, going far beyond the layman's ability to follow. A CEO cannot do that. Part of her job - one of the most important parts - is her ability to communicate what she is doing and to bring people along with her.

There are similar situations in the sporting world. My own success in my sport is at odds with the amount of time and talent that I bring to it. I'm justifiably humble about my riding talent. I'm the wrong shape and my hand-eye coordination, important when jumping, is not very good. I've spent far more of the past 30 years on planes, in meetings and in front of screens than I have on a horse. Yet when I compete I stand a fair chance of being placed in the top five at provincial and national levels. Not always, maybe not even often, but every year I get placed a few times and win once or twice, beating people who devote far more time to the sport.

Learning about focus has made me realise that it's precisely because I have the ability to hold several things in focus at the same time that I can do well in my chosen sport. I relish the complexity: the planning, the training in multiple disciplines, the need to ensure the horse is fit and ready to compete, the constant interaction with farriers, vets, physios, feed merchants, trainers, and a host of others, suits my personality well. All of which means, when I finally ride into the ring or jump out of the cross country starting box, I'm well prepared and my horse is as ready as can be.

The combination of focus and process is the winning combination. Going back to what James Kerr said about the All Blacks in *Legacy*: if you identify what you need to improve, you have defined your focus and you can set goals according to that focus. Then you identify the processes you need to improve to achieve your goal. That sounds simple enough, but it's hard to do and that is where the 5-Step process can help you.

When people struggle to do the 5-Step process it's usually the third step that is trickiest. That is when you choose three themes from your life and do a really deep, very personal brainstorm around each theme. Why do they struggle? I've thought about this a lot. Perhaps it's because choosing a theme may mean restricting your success in other areas. This reluctance to commit to doing a few things exceptionally well becomes obvious when I do the exercise with teams, so I suspect it also comes into play when you go through the process on your own.

Everyone has a dream or had a dream once. When you get to that third step, think about that dream. Are you on the road to achieving it? If yes, then you'll be able to do a great job on Step 3 and you will find working on it really invigorating.

If you once had a dream but you've lost sight of it, that's ok. That might even be why you're reading this book, which is a great step in the right direction. I would say two things to you. Think really hard when you go through Steps 1 and 2. Take account of your whole person. Your dreams may have changed in a good way. Perhaps you wanted to be a rock star as a kid and now you're a hardworking man or woman with a family. Perhaps becoming a rock star was never a realistic dream anyway, as you did not have a guitar, know how to play music or even sing particularly well. As adults we are responsible for attaching our dreams to talents and skills we actually have; kids don't have to do that. When I talk about "dreams" I'm also talking about life as a responsible adult, so it's quite alright to have a theme like "spending more time with the kids" as your top priority. In fact, that is a great one, because it might make you pay attention to focusing better during your working hours so that you can confidently leave in time to have supper with the kids. As a dream it may not be grandiose at first glance, but it's something that could change your future because of the impact it will have on your relationship with your children. The knock-on effect at work could be that by focusing on becoming more efficient, you do your job better and achieve success there as well. As a coach I've worked with many clients on work-life balance and I encourage people to work smarter, not harder. Most of us can work smarter if we try and the outcome is often that we save ourselves time, while others can also see the improvement in their working habits.

Choosing your focus is the key to success.

Chapter 6

Information

Whatever you decide to focus on, you will need to invest in expanding your knowledge in order to get the best possible results. No matter what your goals are, whether they revolve around themes of business, sport, parenting or artistic endeavours, you will find that a wealth of information exists that can help you. Sometimes you need to seek the information and sometimes others bring it to you.

A major theme that emerged from my research was that coaches bring new information to their clients and that this new information often leads to insights. Before they even think about providing any information, coaches listen to their clients. In fact, coaching may be the one place in the world, other than therapy, where people truly listen to your story and your needs. When a coach shares an idea with you, it's because they have understood what might help you. That is invaluable for clients, because not only is it coming from their store of knowledge on management and leadership or their experience of life, but it's coming at the right moment, when the client is open to hearing it.

In case any coaches are reading this book, I'm aware that a purist form of coaching would assert that the client already knows everything they need to know in order to thrive and move past their limiting assumptions. I don't hold strong views either way, but in field research on the coaching process it became clear that coaches often bring important information to their clients that helps their thinking process. That is what I'm trying to do in the first section of this book – share a few challenges that come up again and again in coaching, along with information that can help readers overcome those challenges.

The important thing in coaching is that the client does the thinking and has the insight; the coach is the catalyst for that.

If you don't have a coach, you can still extend your sources of information and there are suggestions for that in the appendix. To achieve your goals you will probably need to expand your knowledge. If you work in the corporate world and you aspire to a senior leadership role, what do you know about leadership? Just because you have an MBA and 15 years of experience, it doesn't necessarily follow that you are a great leader. Are you following current thinking on leadership and the skills and attributes held by great leaders? Do you know what those skills and attributes are and how you stack up against global standards? Or how to develop and integrate them with your own skills and experience? That is the topic of my next book, not this one, but in the meantime, there's plenty of information available on the internet.

Sometimes, what a client needs is the encouragement to dig down and find the information for themselves, and the coach needs to let them do their own research and thinking and not give them too much help. Isaac's story illustrates this (not his real name). We were talking about his frustrations in life and he said, "You know the worst thing is, Sarah, I'm a procrastinator. I want to do things, but I just cannot get started".

As it happens, I'm also a procrastinator, although I've worked hard to address the problem. There are a lot of procrastinators out there; you might even be one yourself. Because I've had to work on it, I know quite a lot about procrastination, but I did not tell Isaac that. Instead, I asked him, "What have you done about it?" Isaac's answer was, "Nothing". "You mean you've got this big problem that you know is holding you back, and you've never done anything about it?" "That's right."

I set Isaac some homework. I suggested he look up procrastination on the internet, learn as much as he could about it and ways of handling it, and asked him to report back to me at the next session. "How did you get on with the research?" I asked. "I couldn't do it", he replied. "I couldn't get started."

There does have to be some spark of motivation if you want to change your life. If you have time to watch TV, scroll through Facebook or read a book, then you have time to research whatever is holding you back. The point is that although procrastination is a difficult and genuine condition, it can be addressed. If you suspect you have it and you have not addressed it, perhaps you could set a theme for the year to research it, understand it and do something about it.

The motivation to get started on that is the first step out of the black hole of procrastination, which is why I'm not giving you any answers here.

> Often, coaches just ask the right question. Such as: "Do you procrastinate?"

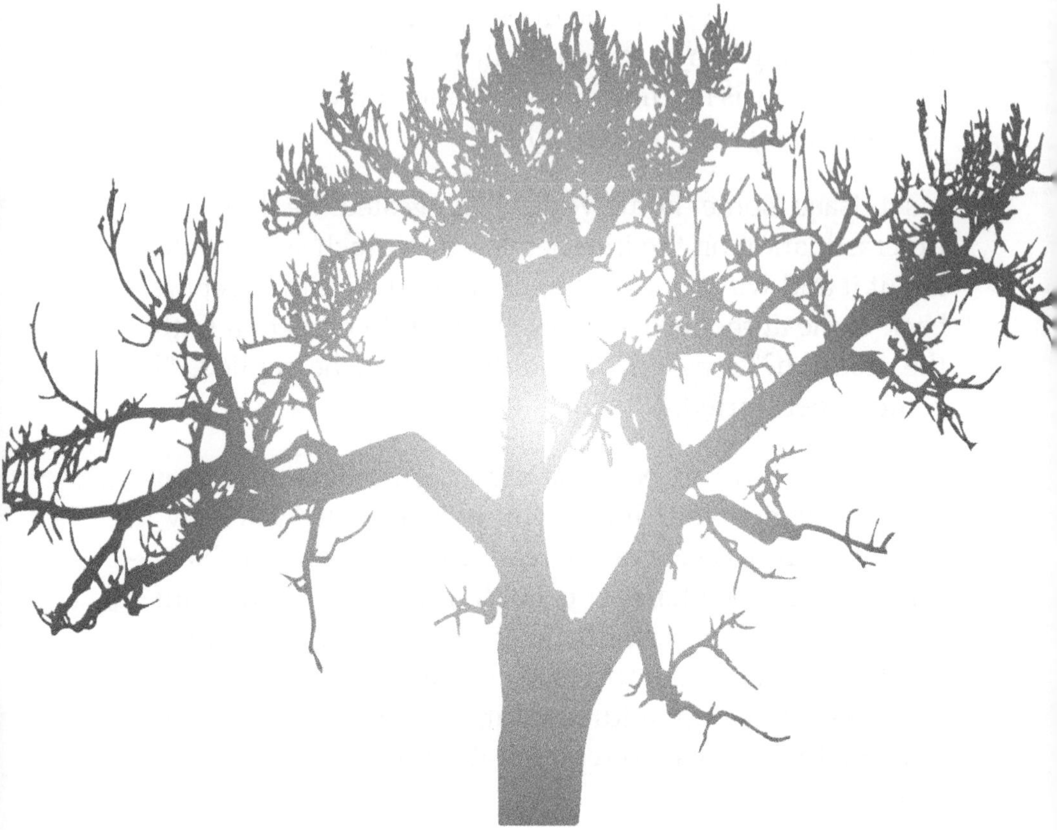

Chapter 7

Learning as adults

Adults in the modern world cannot afford to stop learning; even if you have a business degree or an MBA, you can never stop learning about leadership and management. There are two reasons for this: the first is that classroom learning can only touch the surface of such a deep, complex topic. The second reason is that the body of knowledge on these topics grows and improves all the time. You might not be in a senior leadership position until 10 years after your MBA, but if you did your MBA in 2007, the concept of emotional intelligence and its importance for leaders was only emerging. Social intelligence came even later. Unless you've done extensive reading in the last 10 years, you probably don't know nearly enough about either topic.

There are two famous models for adult learning. The first is the notion that we move from unconscious incompetence to unconscious competence. There's now stacks of research from both neuroscience and behavioural economics that explains how this happens, but the model itself is delightfully simple and resonates with most people.

Unconscious incompetence → Conscious incompetence → Conscious competence → Unconscious competence

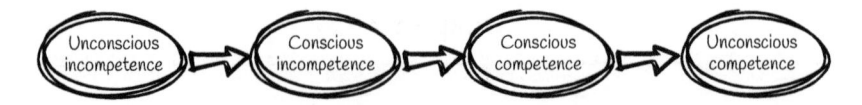

Figure 3: Competency Learning Model

The classic example is that of learning to drive a car which almost everyone does as a young adult. When you first get into a car you have no idea how to drive the thing. That is unconscious incompetence. Most of us then get started and crash a lot of gears, feel nervous on the road, struggle to coordinate everything and feel very clumsy. That is conscious incompetence. With practice (reps!) you become much smoother; you still have to think about what you are doing and concentrate, but you start to find driving quite easy. That is conscious competence. Then at some point, you arrive at your destination and thinking back you realise you can barely remember the driving; it was automatic. That is unconscious competence. Most of us can achieve unconscious competence in many things if we work hard enough to understand what is required and then do the practice. What is much harder is to take it to another level and become really good at what we do. That is where the 10,000 hours combined with lots of focus, good feedback and training come into it.

I was driving my horse to a competition in Port Elizabeth, 10 hours from Cape Town, and gave a friend called Sarah Yeo a lift. Sarah is a new friend and I did not know her very well. I had not really thought about her skills beyond equestrianism. I love how people surprise you. We shared the driving and when she got behind the wheel I instantly realised that she is a very good driver. I don't think I'm a bad driver and I'm certainly confident with a horse trailer, but her driving was in a different class. I asked her about it.

"Oh, I worked for BMW marketing for years and did lots of advanced driving courses and raced a bit as well." Wow! I was not expecting that. It illustrated how taking everyday skills, like driving a car, to a new level requires intense training and a lot of practice, and then challenging the skills in a tough environment like racing. The minute she was behind the wheel, even of my pedestrian Toyota SUV towing a horse trailer, her competence shone through.

The second adult learning model is more complicated and even more valuable. I'll attempt to pique your curiosity by telling you a little bit about it, but it's a huge topic and a lot of books have covered it in detail, so I will not go into the deeper theoretical constructs. If you hunger for them, you can find plenty of sources. The model I describe here was proposed by David Kolb in his classic book, *Experiential Learning*.

Kolb's idea is that we all go through the same process of learning, but we access it from different points, according to our learning style. I might be the kind of person who likes to jump in, try new things and learn from my mistakes. You might be the kind of person who really likes to understand all the theory and to know exactly how something works before you try it. It doesn't matter which kind of learner you are, because the process is circular and we all learn in the end. It does help to understand that people learn differently though, because that increases your social intelligence. If you understand that not everyone on your team will have the same learning style, it will make you more tolerant of the person who seems reluctant to try something new. Maybe they need more information and understanding, and when they have that, they will be only too happy to try out something they've never done before.

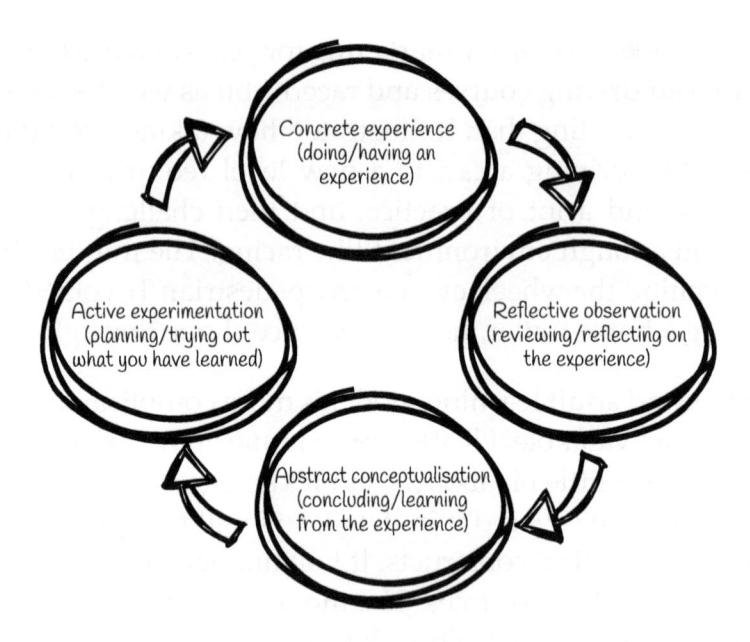

Figure 4: Kolb's learning cycle

Kolb's central idea is that "learning is the process whereby knowledge is created through the transformation of experience". Doing is part of adult learning and it really points to why it's ok to make mistakes, as long as we learn from them. Mistakes should encourage us to reflect on the experience, rather than hide from the opportunity to create new knowledge.

In *Black Box Thinking*, Matthew Syed describes the terrible experience of Martin Bromiley, whose wife died during a routine medical procedure. The hospital was genuinely sympathetic to the family, who were told that "something went wrong with the anaesthesia. These things happen". When Bromiley asked if there would be an investigation he was told there would not: "unless you sue." Doctors are not supposed to make mistakes and medical procedures are not meant to go wrong. When they do and people die, instead of doing a forensic investigation of the incident, the doctors and nurses call the time of death, mourn the tragedy, and move on.

Bromiley came from the airline industry. As you are surely aware, when planes crash they leave behind a "black box". This records everything that takes place in the cockpit during the flight. The actions of the pilots, the autopilot, what they said to one another, and the radio communications. If the plane goes down and the black box is recovered, it's given to investigators. Unlike medical accidents, plane crashes are always investigated. Not only are the accidents investigated, but any learning from the accident will be incorporated into airline procedures and shared with pilots worldwide. The power of the system is incredible, and thousands of lives have been saved because of the aviation industry's ability to address mistakes and learn from them.

Martin Bromiley did not sue the hospital, but he was determined that an enquiry should be held as to the cause of his wife's death. As a result of his persistence an investigation was commissioned, headed up by Michael Harmer, professor of Anaesthetics and Intensive Care Medicine at Cardiff University School of Medicine. The investigation found human error was at fault, and part of the problem was a combination of hierarchy and panic. The report made several key recommendations, and thanks to Bromiley's persistence, surgical procedures have been changed in hospitals throughout the world and many lives have been saved.

If this story, extreme as it is, resonates with you, it's worth thinking about how you respond to mistakes and feedback. Seeing both as a learning opportunity can greatly improve your work, as well as that of your team if you have one. Resistance to learning is often a sign of insecurity, as in the medical profession, so if you do find it hard to hear constructive feedback you might think about where your insecurity comes from and what you can do to address it.

Understanding your own learning style is helpful and there's a useful questionnaire for this. If you look up 'Kolb learning style' online you will easily find a shortened version of it, although the full assessment should be administered by someone who is qualified to put the scores in context.

Once you realise that you can and do need to learn, all you have to do is to decide what to learn. Sometimes it's from experience and sometimes it's from mistakes. Often it's from observing the behaviour of others, both good and bad. You can definitely learn a lot from books, and I have a few suggestions to get you started in the appendix section of this book.

Chapter 8

People are different

Emotional intelligence as a concept has received a lot of attention. Daniel Goleman, the man who coined the term, went on to write about social intelligence, "which, although every bit as important in any situation that involves people, teams and leadership" has received less public attention. Now, however, academic research on social intelligence is starting to throw up some remarkable results, which explain the impact that we have on one another and how we can use social intelligence to motivate ourselves and enjoy our lives more.

From a business perspective, social intelligence is probably the most important quality of senior leaders; more important than pure IQ and perhaps more important than emotional intelligence. Let me give you an example.

While I was President of Western Cape Eventing, one of the things we did as a committee was to bring inspiring world leaders to Cape Town to coach our riders, coaches, and officials. This initiative ended up having an impact beyond the 'coaching the coaches' days, because not only did it inspire the riders and their coaches, it also brought the coaches together on a regular basis, away from the pressure of competitions. They got to know each another better, to understand one another's strengths and weaknesses, and to operate as a team, helping each other as athletes and coaches. The longer term impact was that our province became unbeatable in national competitions. One of our top riders and coaches, Inge Silen, made a comment that really resonated with me. She said, "With this kind of exposure, we may be far from Johannesburg, but we feel very close to the rest of the world". Today international best practices are part of how we train, how we build fences and how our officials operate.

In 2014 we were working on a project to establish the beautiful Kurland Hotel and Polo Estate as a potential venue for the South African Championships. The Fédération Équestre Internationale (FEI), which manages equestrian sports globally, advised us that Eric Winter, one of the world's top course designers and trainers, might be willing to help us. Eric is based in the UK and we had no funds to bring him to South Africa, but a generous friend of the sport contributed her air miles, and the necessary cash, to bring Eric over. That first step led to many benefits. Eric came to Cape Town for the first time in November 2014, he helped design the cross country tracks at Kurland in Plettenberg Bay and he spent two days training our officials. Since then he has returned to South Africa twice a year and become a great friend.

From that first experience I realised that Eric is a quiet genius – he is a humble genius too, so he is not going to like reading those words. He is a consummate horseman and can train people in many dimensions, but his primary focus is cross country course design. He never stops learning, growing and trying new things. In 2017 he was asked to become the course designer for the Badminton Horse Trials, which is the global pinnacle of eventing competitions. Despite attaining these lofty heights, he still comes down to work with us, at our much lower levels, partly because he enjoys the good weather here in February, but mostly because he recognises our desire to learn, improve, and raise our standards.

Eric doesn't need to be the centre of attention and I've often noticed that he will sit quietly, out of the limelight, observing what is going on. There's always a lot of politics around horses, for all sorts of reasons, but Eric manages to avoid becoming embroiled, while helping us who are to better navigate those sometimes tricky waters. He is the embodiment of one of my favourite sayings - we have two ears and one mouth, and we should use them in that proportion. Eric has unusually high social intelligence. He has deep insight into what people are like, and instead of being judgemental or expecting them to change, he uses that insight to help them improve. This, more than all his talent, may well be why he has achieved so much in his career. I learn a huge amount every time I work with him and I'm always humbled, because he reminds me every time, through his actions not his words, that I still have a long way to go in terms of my own social intelligence.

This is important to me because much of what I want to achieve can only be realised with the support and help of others - my family, my friends and my colleagues. That's probably true for you too, so investing in a better understanding of how different we are from one another can help us to achieve our goals.

Social intelligence is a vast, fascinating and complex topic, but it starts with a simple premise - people are different. When we evaluate senior executives one of the key attributes that we assess is social intelligence, and we look at it from many angles. You would be surprised how often senior executives, even CEOs, don't take this seriously, meaning they have never considered their own level of social intelligence, nor how they might improve. Yet the more senior you are as a leader, the more important it becomes.

My research involved talking with focus groups of experienced coaches about that magical moment of insight in coaching, called the "Aha!" moment. My goal was to find out whether we could better understand coaching by using learnings from behavioural economics around decision-making as a theoretical framework. Research already suggested that this approach, called dual processing theory, can help describe what happens in moments of creativity or insight in other fields, so I felt it might also help us to understand what happens in moments of insight during coaching.

The coaches in my focus groups were all experienced business coaches, mostly working with people in the corporate world. As a student of social intelligence for many years, I was not surprised when the discussion revealed that a frequent client insight during coaching sessions is the realisation that "people are different". Many clients have never even considered the idea that other people might be different from them, and that they think differently about life and work. To use a simple example, one of the coaches said:

> "When you wash your dishes, you wash them differently to the way that I would wash them. That's how intricate it is. Our rules of life are not the same. So, in every conversation people need to seek to be heard and also to listen to others, rather than assuming that because this is how I do it then everybody else does it the same way. And that there is no right or wrong way to do it."

Of course, we all believe that our way of washing the dishes is the best way, and I confess that I've never done a survey to identify international best practices in the daily task of dishwashing. I guarantee you one thing, though: the way I do it is not identical to the way that you do it. Now apply that to the many other "rules of life" and consider how different we all are, and then you will realise that social intelligence is basically about seeking to understand those differences and using them to improve our communications with others.

How can you improve your social intelligence? The first thing to do is to focus on it, to think about the people around you, to try to spot ways in which they think differently to you, and to observe how they handle complex situations. Is it different to what you would have done? And was the outcome successful? Seek to identify the people who get the good outcomes and learn from them. In the business world you can probably identify which colleagues or leaders around you are good at smoothing over a meeting or handling awkward people adeptly.

If you're keen to improve your social intelligence I have two suggestions. One is that you observe those kinds of people - what they do, what they say and how they say it. The second suggestion is that when you have a sensitive situation that you need to handle, go to a colleague, a peer or a mentor that you trust, describe the situation, explain how you were thinking of handling it and ask them what they would do, what options they see? As I discussed earlier, we often get stuck in binary choices, but like washing the dishes, handling difficult interpersonal situations, such as office politics, can be done in many different ways. Becoming a student of those possibilities will help you to develop your social intelligence.

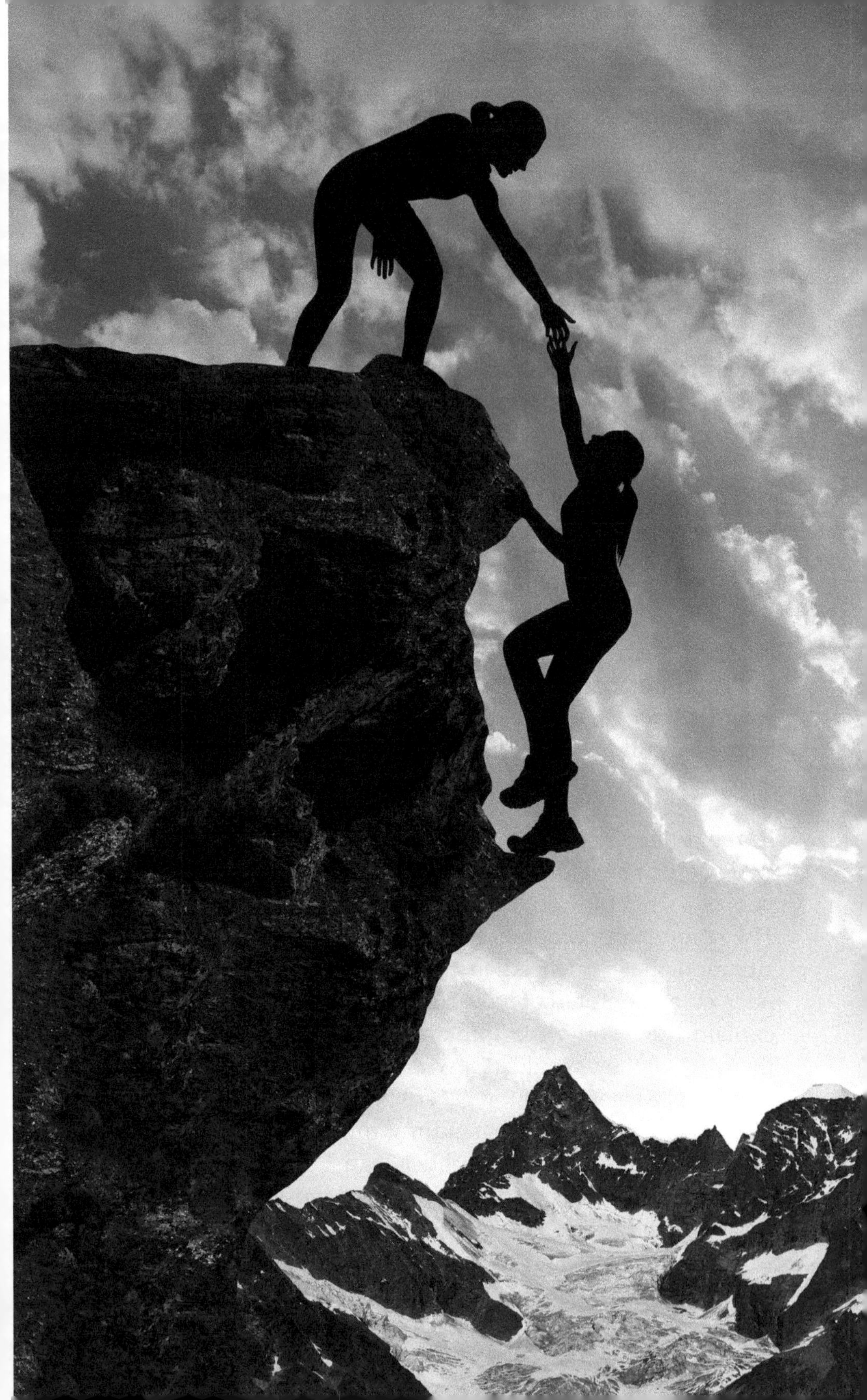

Chapter 9

Humility

I've already talked about humility as a pre-requisite for adult learning. Humility is the first topic in James Kerr's *Legacy*. In the first chapter we learn that the All Blacks clean up the changing rooms after themselves. Even after a great victory in their home stadium, you will find the superstars of New Zealand rugby "sweeping the sheds".

That story had a profound impact on me because it was the moment when I realised that humility and confidence are inextricably linked. To be truly confident one also needs to be truly humble, and one cannot be humble without a certain level of confidence. One of my own most powerful journeys in the past two years has been to identify and try to develop genuine humility; that journey began with *Legacy*. Along with Dr Steve Peter's *The Chimp Paradox*, it's the book I recommend most often.

Lessons don't always come from books, bosses and teachers, however - they often come from clients. When I asked Themba (name changed and an amalgamation of several client stories) to tell me the story of his life, he started telling me how he went to Pretoria University. "No", I said. "I like to start at the beginning. Where were you born?"

So Themba told me he was born in a suburb of Johannesburg called Sophiatown. When he was still a child, the Urban Areas Act of 1955 came into force, preventing black South Africans from living in "white" designated areas. His home was bulldozed in front of the family to ensure that they would never return and they were moved to a black township.

Themba's father had a good job as a driver in Sophiatown, but he could not find work in the new township. Eventually, he went to work in the mines, leaving his family behind. Themba says his mother struggled to raise a large family on the money he sent from the mines. She did her best but the boys ran wild and started getting into trouble.

"How many brothers and sisters do you have?", I asked. "Six", he replied. "And what are they doing now?" "Eish. There were four boys and two girls. My older brother has had problems all his life. I still help him. He drinks and it's very hard for him. I came next and I was able to help the others. My younger brothers have done alright. The next one is an accountant, a senior manager now, and the youngest is an engineer. I am very proud of them. My sisters were different. One is married with her own kids, but she struggles. The other is a schoolteacher with a family. Her husband has done very well, he's an executive at Sasol."

"And what about your mother? Is she still alive?"

"Oh yes."

"She must be very proud of you?"

"Oh, she is, she is proud of all of us. We have bought her a house and I visit her often."

"And your father?" "He died while he was working on the mines. We think it was HIV/Aids, but we cannot be sure. After he died things got very hard for us. I started working, doing anything I could, when I was 12. And in a way, that's what saved me. My mother got a job as a domestic worker and I worked as a garden boy for her employer. But he told me he would only employ me if I did well at school and he helped me. Then I found a study group in the township on a Saturday morning. My mother's employer said I could go and he would still pay me, as long as I came to help in the garden in the afternoon. I learned a lot from that. Hard work, sure, but I also learned that not all rich people are bad. And that helping someone at the right time can change their life."

Themba is exceptionally bright. His school was not particularly good, but he still managed to get into engineering at university and was taken on by a large corporate when he graduated. He has never looked back. He supports the members of his expanding family and encourages the younger members to stay in school and work hard. "It's only a start, but it's the only start", he says.

I've heard many versions of this story during my years in South Africa. I'm amazed and humbled every single time. No-one in my privileged European world ever had to deal with anything like this. Even those who dealt with poverty, illness, or the death of loved ones did not have to deal with all of this with no help from the state, nor support from society.

What shines out from Themba's story is a lack of bitterness. Life dealt him a terrible hand as a child, yet he accepted every opportunity and nothing he said made me feel he was jealous of those who got a better start in life. Sometimes I don't know where to put the feelings I have when I hear stories like this, full of grace and forgiveness. Full of hope for the future.

I'm truly humbled as I listen to such life stories, not only by the story itself, but by the privilege of being the vessel that hears the tale.

On another occasion, I listened to a client describe how his personal success was tinged with sadness because he was unable to pull all his family along with him. At the end of the story our session was over and my client stood up. "I feel so much lighter", he said. "I don't think anyone has ever sat and listened to my story, like you have now." I was touched beyond words and we went on to build a wonderful coaching relationship, where both of us loved our sessions and we explored deep into the heart of things - of life, work, and family.

In my search for humility I learn most from my clients. In coaching we don't tell clients how to do things or how to improve. Instead, we walk along the road with them, for a few months or a few years as their confidante, their sounding board, their trusted advisor. As they open up their world and share their concerns and their challenges, we gain privileged access to how another human being thinks and feels, and how they strive to grow.

The role of coach is wonderful, endlessly challenging and deeply humbling.

Part Two – The 5-Step Process

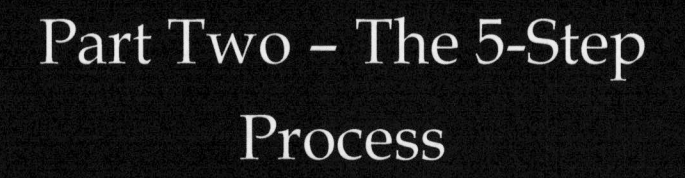

"Life rewards the specific ask and punishes the vague wish."

Tim Ferriss

SMART GOAL

S — Specific
M — MEASURABLE
A — Achievable
R — Realistic
T — Timely

Chapter 10

Setting objectives

The approach that I usually recommend when you set your goals is to use SMART (Specific, Measurable, Achievable, Realistic and Timed) objectives and make a plan to achieve them. Setting SMART objectives really does work.

There's another approach that might also be worth considering.

From reading authors like Grant Cordone and Dr Bob Rotella, I think it might sometimes be worth going for the biggest objectives you can imagine in important areas of your life. In an early eBook that I read on the topic of sports psychology, by Australian eventer Peter Haynes, he described how he aimed for what seemed an impossible dream - that of becoming the Australian eventing champion. Much to his surprise he did become the Australian Champion and afterwards he wished he'd had even bigger dreams, like riding in the Australian team at the Olympics, or even winning an Olympic gold medal.

Dr Rotella makes the point that people rarely exceed their dreams. Tiger Woods wanted to beat Jack Nicklaus's record of winning 18 golfing Masters. He is currently stuck at 14. You could see that as failing to achieve your dreams or you could also describe Tiger Woods as the second-best golfer in the history of the game. And he still has time to achieve his objective; to be the best.

Cordone's suggestion is that we aim for crazy goals, keep them in front of us all the time and then put massive amounts of effort, what he calls 10X, into achieving them. This approach is counterintuitive in some ways. If you want to feel like a winner, you might not want to set crazy objectives that you are not likely to achieve. Then again, if you want to go beyond what you even think is possible, why not try?

This year I'm going to play with a different idea. I'm taking two of my most important objectives and expanding them significantly. My 10X might not be Cordone's but I'm prepared to put everything I've got into these two goals. And the older I get the more ambitious I get, because my time gets more limited.

When I turned 50 I told myself that I wanted the next 25 years to matter as much as the past 25, if not more.

I make that point in terms of goal setting because I'm currently driven by this timing, and drawing confidence from the fact that I've reached my half century as fit, healthy and ambitious as ever. Your life will be in a different place, so choose what works best for you. Some years we need to be realistic about what we can accomplish. Any working mother with small children that I know is way too busy to set crazy objectives. She is already doing exceptionally well to be holding down a job, rearing children and trying to have some kind of personal life, so the 10X goals can probably wait a bit.

Instead, what she might need is time for regular, weekly exercise, so she can build fitness and have some time to herself.

I firmly believe that you can have everything in a lifetime – well, maybe not everything, but an awful lot - just not all at the same time.

Choose your moment to set 10X goals.

One of the main benefits you'll get from sitting down quietly for an hour and going through this process is that you'll have a chance to reflect on what is important to you and to develop a plan to achieve it.

Just because you want something doesn't automatically mean you will get it. If your dreams are ambitious, are you really prepared for the work and sacrifices it will take to achieve them?

Running a marathon sounds great. Getting up at 4am on a winter's morning to put the miles in before work is a lot less fun. One thing is certain though - if you don't aim to run that marathon and if you don't put the plan in place, then you'll never do it. And you may surprise yourself. Once you get into the habit of training, when that winter morning comes maybe nothing will stop you from getting up and out there.

In Part Three I have some suggestions to help keep you from going astray.

Life is full of the unexpected and sometimes it can get between you and your dreams. For example, I compete seriously in my sport and for that I need my horse to be fit and capable. If he gets injured, we are not going to achieve our objectives for the year and there's nothing I can do about it.

Similarly, if your dream was to get the promotion you've always wanted but the business goes through a serious downturn and you get retrenched, that is most likely going to be a horrible experience and it will also mean the end of that particular dream, for now.

That doesn't have to be a disaster; it just means we have to be flexible and prepared to adjust when the unexpected happens.

Alta's Story

I met Alta in February 2016 when we started the MPhil programme at Stellenbosch University Business School. Alta was looking forward to 2016. She worked in a senior HR role in a big company and to help her career progress she signed up for a course in Executive Coaching. Doing this programme was her dream.

Alta started the course in February, enthused and excited about the year ahead. At the start of the second module in March, she was a different person. She'd just been retrenched after 22 years of working for the same company. She was completely shocked; her friends wondered if she would get over it.

To everyone's surprise, she did, and faster than expected. She always had a passion for the environment and wanted to do something that would have a positive impact. She got together with a colleague who had also been retrenched and they identified a range of products aimed at helping the environment and they started importing them.

The business is doing well, and Alta is having the most fun she's ever had in her life. She's been through some ups and downs in her personal life, but she loves the business, the challenges it brings, and the positive impact it's having on the environment.

Some of the products are specifically aimed at water saving, and as Cape Town faces a severe drought, Alta and her colleagues are proud of the positive contribution they are making. Change is painful, but it often leads to positive outcomes; it certainly did for Alta. In December 2017, she was one of a small cohort who graduated from the programme in the shortest possible time, another achievement of which to be proud.

The 5-Step Process

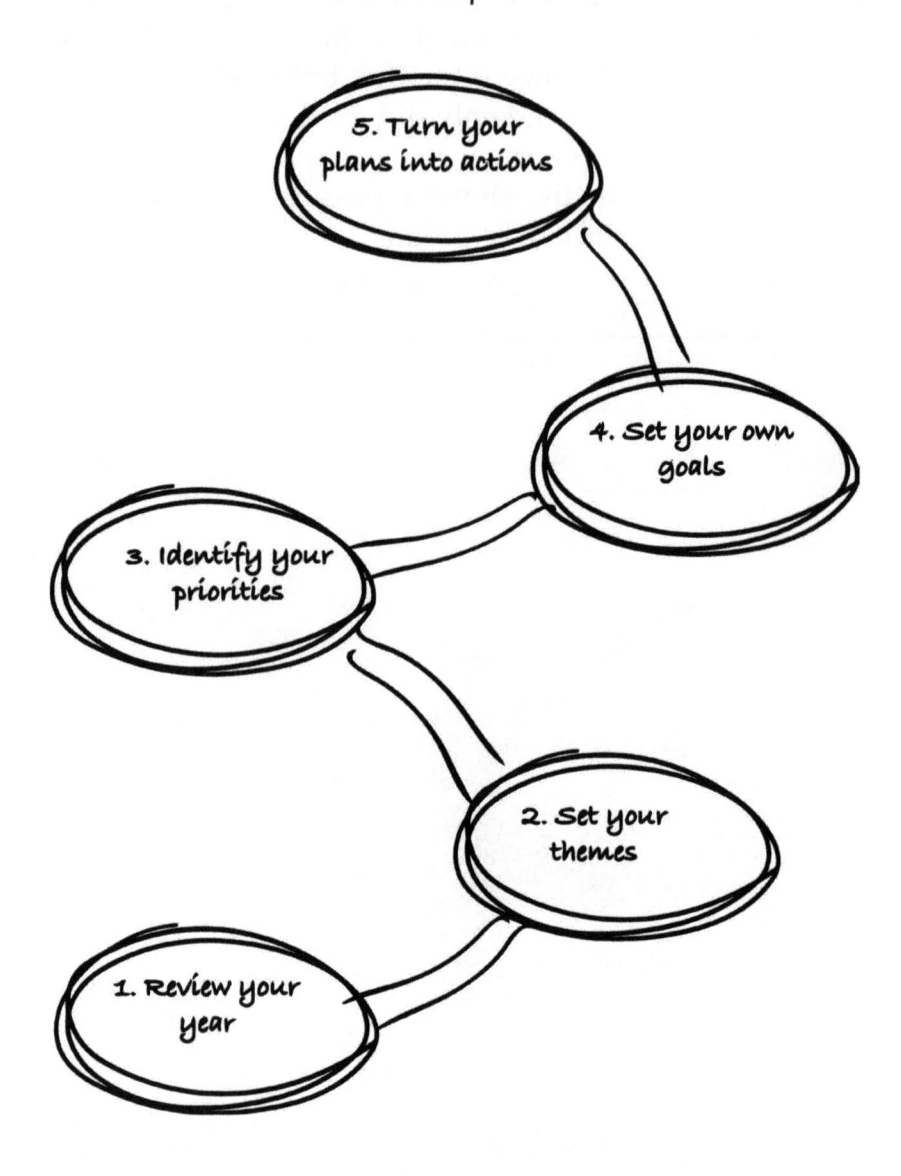

- 5. Turn your plans into actions
- 4. Set your own goals
- 3. Identify your priorities
- 2. Set your themes
- 1. Review your year

Chapter 11

Planning can change your life

The 5-Step Plan

Setting the right number of SMART (Specific, Measurable, Achievable, Realistic and Timed) objectives and putting a schedule in place to achieve them really does work. If you want to throw in a couple of really big multipliers and see if that helps to stretch you, then try it. I'm doing it this year, but only on two of my objectives. All the rest are SMART.

There are a lot of great books and theories out there to help you achieve your goals. What's different about this one? This approach is not just about helping you to achieve your goals; it's about getting your focus right so that your goals align with your values and what really matters to you now. Sometimes you might be surprised by what you find out about yourself. Let me give you an example of what I mean.

I sat down in January to plan my year, as I have done every year since I discovered this 5-Step approach.

The last 12 months had been great in many areas (I'll share more about that in a moment), but I had to admit that study had taken a toll on my relationship with my husband. When I sat down and did Step 3 of the 5-Step plan, which is where you choose your themes for the year, I thought about my whole life. Normally I prioritise my work and my competitive sport and set ambitious goals in both areas. For the past two years achieving my study goals was also important and I was very pleased that I had completed the programme in the minimum possible time. Thinking about this year's themes, work had to be at the top of the list as I'm setting up a new partnership with some pretty demanding targets. This book was second on the list. I thought that getting it published would be really hard, but in fact I was introduced to my publishers, Knowledge Resources, in February, and they immediately said they'd liked it, so my priority shifted to getting it ready for publication.

The third theme was obviously my riding objectives. Or was it? As I sat and brainstormed I realised that setting ambitious riding objectives this year would just put pressure on me and take my focus off what really matters. I'm now at a level where I can comfortably compete at a notch below my ultimate target, build some experience, enjoy my competitions and not worry about it too much. We might have a great year, we might not, but I decided to take the pressure off and spend more time with my husband, Peter. I worked on that as a theme instead. That is quite a personal theme so I'm not going to share much more about it. I will tell you one thing though - from the moment that I wrote down "Prioritise Peter's happiness", things shifted in our relationship. Better communications, more thoughtfulness from both of us, those kinds of things. Writing things down is the first step to committing to them and it really does make a difference.

Whoever you are, think about this as you set your themes for the year. If your kids are growing up fast and you're not spending enough time with them, prioritise that. If you need to address health issues, then that is at the top of the list. If you need to sit down and think about your finances, good, this is the time to figure that one out. Maybe its planning your dream holiday. Fine, even if it takes more than a year to save enough, commit to it now.

If you're at the stage of your life where you want to focus on your business and career themes and go big on those, great, do it! But still take the time to think of your whole life and make sure you're not missing something deeply important, even if it may seem more day-to-day, or pedestrian.

Step 1 prepares the ground for Steps 2 and 3. These are often the most challenging, and rewarding, steps in the whole process. Step 2 is where you choose your focus. This sets the stage for everything else that happens to you this year, so enjoy the process and engage in it with all your heart.

This does not take long to do. Take the time to think about yourself holistically. Take account of every aspect of your life: work, home, finances, family, sport, health, fitness and anything else that is important.

All you need is a pen, a notepad, a cup of coffee and a quiet hour to yourself.

Ready to begin?

Step 1 - Review the past year

1. Review your year

Take a notepad and write down what you've achieved in the year. Think about things like:

- ambitions, achieved or not;
- creative work;
- new skills you've developed or new behaviours you have learned;
- work successes;
- your network: people you met or got to know better;
- places you visited;
- things you achieved at home;
- your health;
- family highlights.

Now write down any disappointments. Things like:

- setbacks at work;
- health issues you've had to deal with;
- moments where you had to change plans or faced difficulties;
- blocks or hurdles to achieving what you want;
- financial or practical challenges;
- difficult family or friend situations.

If you did this exercise last year, now is the time to look back at last year's plan. Compare what you aimed to achieve with your actual achievements.

Next, write a headline for the last 12 months.

If you were being interviewed and were asked to describe the year, what would you say? Don't be too hard on yourself – sometimes it's the journey that's important, not always the goals.

Step 1 – My review of 2017

To help you, here is my review of 2017. I've taken out some of the more personal themes but this gives you an idea of what you should be thinking about. Re-reading it as I include it here, I can see I'm quite tough on myself. That's ok, it's who I am. The language of this is quite informal and so should yours be; this is your own document and is not really meant to be shared.

Sarah's review of 2017

MPhil done. Tick. So pleased about that. And a really respectable mark. Learned a lot, really enjoyed it. Glad it's over.

Business – well that went around the houses a bit. I had set what I thought was quite an ambitious financial goal for the year, and to my surprise when I added it up I ended up hitting my earnings goal which is great as it was always my aim at the back of my mind.

Learned that I couldn't work with one potential partner. She's an amazing person and I admire her at many levels, but we are not the right team. I'm quite sad about that as

I think that together we are really powerful in front of clients and could work at literally any level. But it's not meant to be. She helped me earn some real money and I'm grateful for that.

Also came to the realisation that my other potential client is not going to work out. It's a pity as they were so enthusiastic about it at the beginning, but I realise that they cannot deliver on their ambitions. I would really enjoy working with them but sounds like the organisation is struggling to handle their new businesses and the restructuring.

I learned a lot by contacting the players in this field. Was a great project and really helped me refine what I want out of life. Meeting people who asked tough and challenging questions was humbling and above all made me realise what an extraordinary life we lead and how lucky we are.

Glad that my sleepless nights led me to contact Andrew [Woodburn, my partner in our new venture]. This looks like the real thing and I am so excited about it. This could turn out to be 2018's biggest success.

My relationship with my coaching clients is wonderful. Amazing to work so closely with such incredible people. Very excited that most of them want to continue working with me in 2018, looking forward to an interesting journey.

The book - didn't get far on it in 2017 except that academic writing has sharpened and clarified my thinking and I'll deliver the new version before the end of Jan 2018.

And I really like the way it's headed, I think there's a real book in there and this version is enough to show agents and see if I can find a proper publisher. Will be setting that as a 2018 objective.

Airbnb has turned into a nice solid little breadwinner.

Am a bit annoyed that I wasted some of the money on LinkedIn, but I needed to play with their marketing tools to see what they could do. Result: it's not for me at the moment but it was good to play with the technology.

I am not sure how we grow the Airbnb - might be better to spend some money on the house if we have some, put in the bathrooms and upgrade the kitchen and see if it can be a "perfect hideaway". Not sure it can - might take more money than it's worth. Not an important priority going forward but has been great to have it.

Filipe [my horse] - 2017 didn't turn out as the year that I'd hoped with two cross country falls that bruised my ego more than anything else and mean a possible downgrade. BUT I have figured out the tying up thing [tying up is a muscle spasm problem in horses, more formally known as azoturia] and how to help him with travelling. Realise he needs a lot of care and attention if the weather is too hot or too cold. And we had some very nice wins and some improvement in our elementary dressage marks all of which are taking us on the right track. We came second in the 2017 amateur championship which was really encouraging. [We compete against professionals, so this is a way of measuring ourselves against our real peers: other amateur riders.]

A side part of that is my own diet and fitness, not so great in 2017. Really good up to September and then I let it go and here I am five kg heavier which is a lot on my little frame. I feel quite gross but also quite determined to work on it and to apply my new "it's the process" philosophy to my dieting and exercise. On the health front, if this funny bloat doesn't clear up completely with a regime and 5:2

then a doctor's appointment is top priority. Also make sure I do the tests that I need to get done.

Headline for 2017

MPhil eventer struggles with building new business but doesn't give up

That is it. It was a year when I nailed most of my goals, but didn't feel a huge sense of accomplishment so I'm aiming for much more in 2018.

Step 2 - Set your themes for this year

2. Set your themes

Steps 2 and 3 are the really fun part of this entire process. Step 2 delivers the most important outcome – where you should focus your efforts. Even if you don't see yourself as a creative person you'll find this part invigorating and even creative, because it's intrinsically interesting to you and that helps you concentrate. You are setting themes first: general areas of life where you want to focus your attention and, this is important, bring about change.

We're not looking at specifics here: use your reflections on the past year to help you set your themes for this year.

Write down the three areas of your life you want to focus on this year.

Not more than three. If you achieve them early you can add more, but for now focus on just three themes.

Here are some suggestions to kick start your thinking process:

Work; business; money; leadership; skill development; work/life balance; time-management; productivity; fitness and health; family and friends; fun; travel and exploration; home; love and relationships; giving back.

Step 2 – example

For my three themes in 2018 I chose:

- building the new business;
- getting my book published; and
- prioritising Peter's happiness.

Step 3 - Identify your priorities

3. Identify your priorities

Now you're going to brainstorm by inducing a state of "flow" that should allow you to become more creative and move you to a deeper state of thinking about your themes. This might sound unlikely, but concentrating really hard on one thing for five minutes brings about a creative, reflective state of mind that should lead you to make interesting new connections and ideas.

Take a piece of paper and a pen. Write down your first theme and for at least five minutes (set the timer on your phone) jot down ideas about how your life could be better a year from today. Concentrate on outcomes - the best possible outcomes you can imagine. This is the time to dream.

Keep the pen moving, draw as well as write, get it all down. Don't lift the pen from the page for the whole five minutes.

> I use Evernote as my online notebook, though I also have a paper notebook I bring to meetings. For this exercise, I use pen and an old fashioned A4 pad. When I did this last year I lost my paper sheets, so this time I photographed them when I was finished and added them to Evernote. That way I now have everything together when I come to review the year.

As you do this exercise remember to be ambitious; put no limits on what you could achieve.

Build on your ideas. If you want to be creative, what does it look like? A book, a painting course or finding a way to take your team to a new level of delivery?

Keep less glamorous objectives in mind; maybe you need to address some aspect of your health or well-being?

Try to be specific – it's not "get fit", it's run 15km a week or walk the Otter Trail. Think about outcomes – the best outcomes you can imagine. Thinking about outcomes is the clever thing about this exercise, because it helps to crystallise what you really want and gets it into words. Be bold and brave at this point. You can refine it later; for now, dream up the best possible outcomes.

> Now do the same for the next two themes.

You should find this process exciting and invigorating and it might be that one of the priorities starts to take precedence. That is good news because it means the exercise is helping you to prioritise better.

Ideas might emerge that surprise you. This exercise can be a way of tapping into your subconscious; of pulling out the ideas you've had over the last year but forgotten as other more urgent thoughts take over. Do not reject any surprising thoughts - they may be the important ones.

Some people have dreams that appear huge and aspirational: write a book; earn a million Rands or Dollars; start a PhD. Other people's dreams might not appear so demanding: lose weight; get fit; learn to cook really well; take a dream vacation. Does it matter? Of course not. These are *your* dreams. If you've always wanted to be a better cook, then that is your dream. Succeeding might lead to expanding your dream or to many happy, confident hours in the kitchen. Do not allow other people to influence *your* dream - decide for yourself. If you *do* want to write a book, fantastic, this is the tool for you too.

> When you've done all three, take a short break.

> Deliver the book to clients and friends as an ebook with beautiful design by the end of January. Ask M who her friend is who can help me with illustrations and design. I won't have time to do that part myself, learning the tools takes too long. Going to be a big cost.
>
> Use that to find a publisher to publish it by the end of 2018. How do I do that? Ideas that come to mind right now are find an agent - look online there must be some. Who in SA publishes business books? Who published Salome's book?
>
> Make it a bestseller - well that's kind of a joke as it's unlikely but at least research the elements that go into a good book and keep doing that. Even if I find a publisher keep working at that because they will never care as much as I do.
>
> Marketing ideas well if I get it published I need to figure out the best way to market it and make sure it gets attention. My own social networks, and asking friends to help with the amazon part. And book launches. And promoting it - maybe M can help with this need to see what she would charge
>
> Design - need to keep thinking about design and keep on thinking about what works in design very important.
>
> Book launches, could have some fun with that, see if we can get lots of friends to come
>
> Find an agent who loves my work? How to go about doing that, need to flesh out that idea. Start writing the next book be proactive. Talk to people I know who have published but I don't know if they are willing to share contacts, can but try. Wiley is an obvious one, but UK based and my stories are so SA? Also KR - see they publish people who's books I've read.
>
> Having a book will be great for speaking gigs and to share with clients going forward. Really cool, this is something I want to do.

Figure 5: Example of a dream sheet

The page that I'm sharing is based on the page I used to think about how I would get the book published. The amazing thing about this theme was that it fell into place so quickly. In the first two weeks of January I worked on getting an eBook out for my friends and clients, then a new acquaintance introduced me to Knowledge Resources. They like books that are ready to go, so they gave me some feedback and offered to publish almost immediately. I went back to work straightaway to incorporate their feedback and develop some more material in places. Once I had got that far, I went back to my themes and started thinking, "What next? How do I use this published book to support my other objectives?"

I'm using a personal example but there's a powerful message here. The minute you write something down as a goal, you start moving towards it. In a Californian study, Dr Gail Matthews looked at a varied group of professionals and divided them up simply by whether they wrote down their goals. Astonishingly, those who wrote down their goals were 42% more likely to achieve them. I've seen how true this is. I've always wanted to publish a book, but this is the first time in my life that I've specifically written down: "Get my book published" as a goal. If I had not made that written commitment, I probably would not have mentioned my book to Debbie Goodman of Jackhammer in Cape Town. She immediately, and very kindly, introduced me to Knowledge Resources.

I cannot stress this enough: when you write something down and commit to it, you have already started to make it come true. Why? Because your attention zeroes in on it without you even realising. You start to focus, explicitly, on what you want. That is why it's so important to spend time on Steps 2 and 3 choosing the right themes for your year and to brainstorm the outcomes you want and what they look like. Once you circle those and create your objectives around them in Step 4, you are well on the road to successfully achieving them. This sounds extraordinary, but it's true.

Before we move on let me share one of my favourite stories with you. There's a gnarly old US equestrian star called Denny Emerson. He has continued to ride well into his 70s, and he has written a wonderful book: *How Good Riders Get Good*. In it he tells the story of the flea jar, which, in my own words, goes like this:

If you get a large jar and put some fleas in it, the fleas will try to jump out of the jar. If the jar has a lid on it, the fleas will bang their little heads against the lid and they obviously will not be able to escape from the jar. After a while they still jump, but they don't jump high enough to bang their heads, because they've learned that they cannot get out of the jar. Now here is the thing. If you then take the lid off the jar, the fleas will never jump out; they have learned their lesson and they stay confined to the jar until one day, sadly, they die in the jar.

Too often we can be like that. We think we are confined and we don't reach too high for fear of banging our heads. We limit our choices. When I first raised the topic of choices in Chapter 2, I described how we narrow our frames and limit ourselves to binary choices when there could be many more options available to us. Broadening our frames and being really creative about our options is like building ourselves a bigger jar.

I often tell this story when I give motivational speeches about leadership and transformational change. The topic sounds grand, but really it's about helping people to understand that they have far more power than they realise to change their lives, if they really want to. The story of the flea jar is a powerful illustration of how we become trapped by our day-to-day lives and it's the story people talk about when they see me again. They will say: "I've got a bigger jar."

Step 4 – Set your goals for the year

4. Set your own goals

After the break, return to your "dream" sheets and circle the ideas and objectives that jump out at you or seem the most important, or both. You want to feel inspired and excited and you want these things to have a positive impact on your life.

Now write them down as a list.

Aim for about three objectives per theme – a maximum of nine. If it's a big one – like earning an important new qualification – you can focus on just that area. You should end up with three to nine objectives.

> Now start to break those objectives down into tasks or create a schedule that will start you on the road to achieving them.

Maybe it's just me, but I find this bit quite hard. This is where you turn your theme into objectives and then a real plan. I tend to overload my life. I think it's because the parts of my life are very different and switching quickly between them can be a challenge.

What are those parts?

1. Wife, housekeeper, stepmother, step-granny, daughter and sister (family is always the most important to me).
2. Coach to senior executives, specifically public company CEOs.
3. Partner in a start-up leadership services business.
4. Our social life - time for friends and family.
5. Competitive rider.
6. Running a thriving Airbnb business.

Though they might take up time, some of these don't belong on my list of themes. Take the Airbnb business; I've run it for a couple of years now. The advantage of the platform is that it handles the bookings and the money. It also reminds you when guests are arriving, so there's no risk of forgetting a booking. We've turned this into an efficient process that fits seamlessly into managing our household. I might want to grow it at some point, but it doesn't need to be a priority this year. We consistently get five-star reviews and our business is growing, despite the competition. We are Superhosts, which proves that our process is working well. That aspect of our farm life doesn't need more attention this year.

> Some of your objectives will need you to change your habits, so make sure you don't try to achieve too much at once.

For example, if you want to exercise regularly, set a schedule you can live with and stick to it. If you cannot stick with it, make it easier or try a different form of exercise - one that appeals to you more - and keep trying until you can stick to it.

If you want to write a book or complete a thesis, commit to a writing programme that works for you. It might only be a paragraph before you go to bed, but make sure you commit to a process, and then stick to it.

I have a busy life and I can find this exercise overwhelming. If you find yourself in the same situation, here is what I've learned over the years. Forcing yourself to focus on your priorities - the things that you really want to achieve - can help you to declutter the rest of your life or deprioritise some things until your top priority hits target.

This reluctance to focus is especially true when I do this exercise with teams. They come up with such great ideas and outcomes in Step 3 that they don't want to refine them down to just three themes and three objectives in Step 4. Yet if they don't, the focus dissipates and they struggle to achieve anything at all.

I've learned that it's better to ask them to choose one or two themes that need a long-term focus in order to be successful, then one or two themes where they believe they can deliver quickly. If they deliver, they can bring in a new theme; if they don't, they need to go back and understand the roadblocks and see if they can solve them or find a workaround.

Here is an example of how I prioritised one of my themes when a big roadblock appeared, and how I managed to stay focussed.

In 2017, my most important objective was to complete my studies and graduate by the end of the year. We were warned that this would be a huge challenge, and that most candidates don't finish their theses in time to graduate within the required two years.

By August I realised that I needed a lot of research hours to finish by the end of September. At the same time, a lucrative work project arrived. I felt completely overwhelmed. I sat down and looked at my objectives, then I saw the solution. I simply deprioritised my sport. I did not stop, but I accepted that I was not going to hit my sporting objectives for the year.

The impact of this was extraordinarily liberating, and having reprioritised, I nailed my most important objectives by the end of the year.

That is the beauty of this process; it doesn't just help you set your objectives at the start of the year, it also helps you to prioritise what is most important as the year goes by. If you start feeling overwhelmed, you can use it to figure out what is most important and narrow down your focus. Conversely, if things are swinging along nicely, you can increase your scope and push yourself to achieve more.

Here are my objectives for 2018. I've included my two business themes but excluded the personal one - it's a little too personal.

My new business	The book
o Set a really ridiculous 10x target just for fun to see if it proves the point about writing it down gets you closer to a bigger target – if I think we can do R1 Million, make it R10 Million	o Deliver the ebook with a beautiful design for friends and clients by the end of Jan
o Aim to average 2 new bookings per month for assessment and 1 new really senior coaching client per month	o Get the book published – need to break this one down into list of tasks
o Carry out at least two major Board assessments in 2018, preparing the ground for more in 2019. Start thinking about the kinds of people we need to hire in year two	o Make book a bestseller! Kind of a joke but why not write it down – 10x it. Definitely should say market the book and have fun doing that through talks and media.

Figure 6: Sarah's objectives

Apps that can help you

I find mobile apps useful to help me achieve my objectives.

1. **Hey Jude**: I first learned about virtual assistants from Tim Ferris in *The Four-Hour Week*, but I couldn't figure out the best way to use them. Last year a friend told me about Hey Jude, which is a virtual assistant that helps with all those smaller, more urgent tasks that need to be done today - things that would often go on your 'To Do' list, like remembering to send a present to someone, to make a restaurant reservation or to book a doctor's appointment. Or realising as you are on the way to the airport that you need to book a car because originally you thought you would use Uber, but actually a car would be better (this happens to me a lot as I commute between the Cape and Johannesburg).

    Send Jude a message and Jude will take care of it.

    The great thing is that it costs ZAR200 a month, so you can afford it. Hey Jude is available in South Africa, some other African countries, the United Arab Emirates, the United Kingdom, Ireland, Australia and New Zealand. Some months I don't use it much, but when I get really busy, it's invaluable.

    What I love about it is that I tend to write my "To Do" list late at night or early in the morning when the doctor's offices or the restaurants are closed, and I don't feel like getting onto my laptop to send a message. Now those tasks don't even go onto my list as Jude sorts them out for me. Tick. Done. Time saved.

    Hey Jude has also launched a business service with a lot more options, such as preparing presentations, proofreading and other useful services. If I end up using it this year I will report back. In the meantime, I'm finding their personal service useful and affordable.

2. **Audible**: It took me a while to get into audio books, then I realised they are great company on long drives – and South Africa is a large country. They are good company out running too, or even on holiday when you want to read, but you also want to look at the place. Above all audio books allowed me to increase the number of books I read, which is great as I'm constantly on a quest for new information. I like business books and autobiographies. Recently I listened to the autobiographies of both Richard Branson and Arnold Schwarzenegger. Curiously enough, though I enjoyed Branson's book, I could relate to Schwarzenegger's more and I found it much more inspiring. I've shared some insights from Schwarzenegger, and how Tim Ferriss piqued my interest in him, earlier in this book.

3. **Pomodoro**: This is a straightforward but very useful timer. Science suggests that short breaks refresh us and improve the quality of our output. What is clever about Pomodoro is that it gives you 25-minute blocks of time, then suggests you take a 5-minute break. After two hours, it suggests a longer break. When you are trying to focus on big tasks like writing reports, this is helpful. I also find it keeps me honest about how I spend my time. It's easy to sit at my desk for five hours and think I've done five hours of productive work, but as I only set the Pomodoro clock when I get really stuck into the task, I might find I've only done five or six 25-minute chunks of time.

4. **Evernote:** A really handy Notebook app that sits on your laptop as well as your devices. I use the free version and find it more than adequate for my needs. It's

handy because it syncs to all your devices, you can drag and drop emails and photos, even email attachments, and you can set up a Notebook for every project. The search function is terrific - if you can't remember which Notebook you wrote something in, you just search for it. Notebooks are also projects that can be shared with others, so it can be useful for teamwork. As I said above, I do like to use pen and paper and I sometimes photograph the page and drop it into the Evernote Notebook. I try lots of apps and then abandon them, but Evernote has stuck.

5. **Running apps**: I try to run three times a week, and it's quite easy to think I achieved that when I really did not. Now I use an app called Wahoo Fitness to record my runs. Lots of people prefer Strava, which links to multiple devices, watches and heart monitors. These apps work in similar ways - they measure your routes, heart rate and speed, which is enough for me, though they can do much more. The front page gives me my running history for the last four weeks, so it keeps me honest.

6. **Airbnb**: We joined Airbnb a couple of years ago. We have two cottages on the farm that we had done up for a big family wedding that were not being used, so I thought I would give it a try and it's been a great success. I love the platform because it takes care of the reservation, the money, and reminds you when guests are coming to stay. Early on we worked out how to get 5* reviews and be Superhosts. At a time when I was working less because I was studying, it was a welcome source of revenue. We have lovely guests - the kind of person who books a farm stay through Airbnb is generally compatible with us. I mention Airbnb specifically in case you find yourself in a situation

where you need to generate more income quickly and have suitable accommodation that you are not using. Airbnb is well worth a try.

Now, let's turn those plans into actions...

Step 5 - Turn your plans into actions

5. Turn your plans into actions

Take a calendar and mark up the commitments you already have in place.

Choose one objective from your list. Now write down what you must do in January, February and March, i.e. the first quarter of the year, to be on track to achieve that goal by the end of March.

If it will take longer, spread your actions throughout the year but make a detailed first quarter plan.

Now start breaking up the themes into objectives and ideas and put them into buckets, like Colette did in Chapter 1. That will make it easier to think about the actions and processes needed to achieve those goals. This year I'm starting a new business and there's a lot I don't know yet about how it's going to work, so the bucket exercise was very helpful. Here it is.

Chapter 11: Planning can change your life

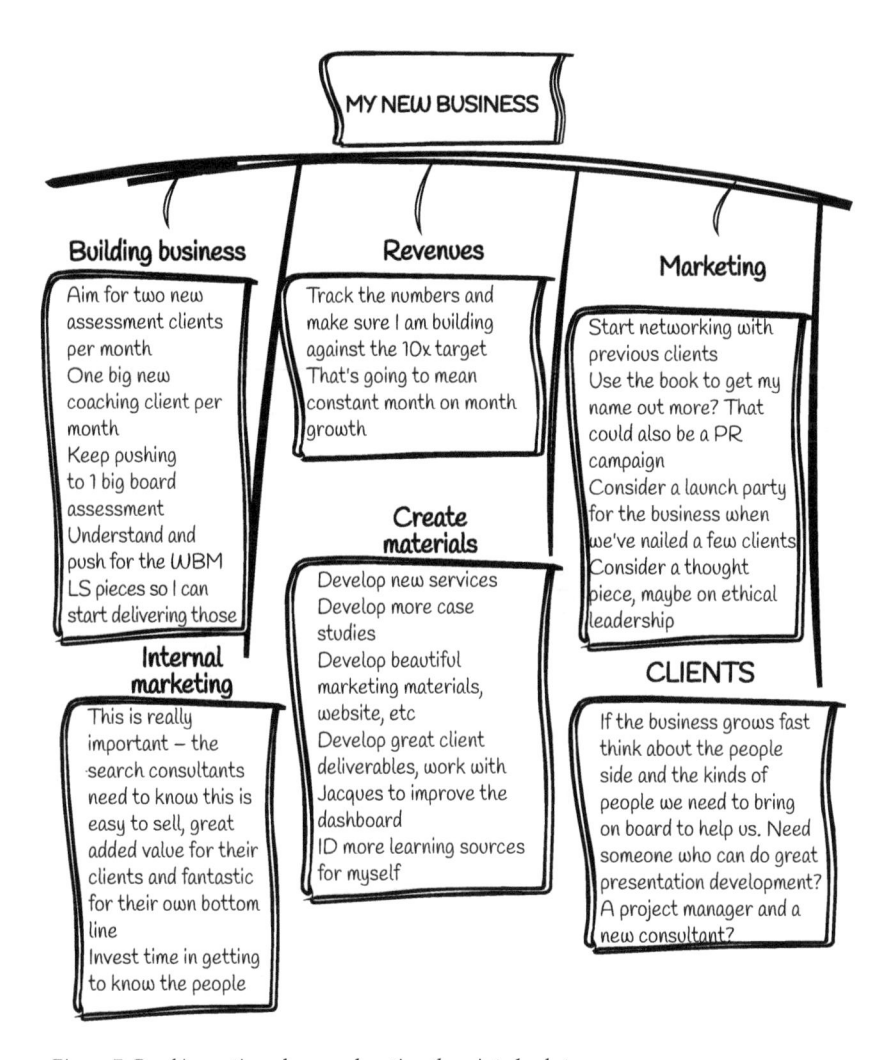

MY NEW BUSINESS

Building business
- Aim for two new assessment clients per month
- One big new coaching client per month
- Keep pushing to 1 big board assessment
- Understand and push for the WBM LS pieces so I can start delivering those

Revenues
- Track the numbers and make sure I am building against the 10x target
- That's going to mean constant month on month growth

Create materials
- Develop new services
- Develop more case studies
- Develop beautiful marketing materials, website, etc
- Develop great client deliverables, work with Jacques to improve the dashboard
- ID more learning sources for myself

Marketing
- Start networking with previous clients
- Use the book to get my name out more? That could also be a PR campaign
- Consider a launch party for the business when we've nailed a few clients
- Consider a thought piece, maybe on ethical leadership

Internal marketing
- This is really important – the search consultants need to know this is easy to sell, great added value for their clients and fantastic for their own bottom line
- Invest time in getting to know the people

CLIENTS
- If the business grows fast think about the people side and the kinds of people we need to bring on board to help us. Need someone who can do great presentation development? A project manager and a new consultant?

Figure 7: Breaking actions down and sorting them into buckets

The next thing I did was to create a simple one-page chart for the year. I've put my current objectives in here. When you do this, you can have a whole page for each month if you want. What you'll see is that you'll have quite a clear idea of what to do for the first few months, and then it gets a bit vaguer. That's fine, as long as you go back and flesh out the later months as they draw nearer. That can be very motivating because you'll see how many "small wins" are already in place. On this page I've included commitments that are in already in place, like travel and competitions, so I can clearly see how easily they fit into my planning or if they actually just get in the way. This really helps you to prioritise. Here is how mine looks.

January
- Get the new book out
- Start clearing the decks for the launch of the new business

February
- Spend at least two weeks in Joburg
- See if we can book first piece of business before month end
- Eventing mid-month
- CWB coming to stay
- Airbnb very busy
- Develop initial marketing materials and familiarise myself with WBM systems
- Win first piece of business!

March
- AW in CT first week
- Spend at least two weeks in Joburg
- New coaching client
- New assessment business
- Work on materials – commit to delivering new LSI look and feel and design
- Eventing mid-month
- Bush with Allan for Easter

April
- Spend at least two weeks in Joburg
- Committed to Mashutu trip mid-month, will probably have to cancel
- Speaking engagement
- Two new assessment clients
- Board assignment?
- Status of materials
- Eventing in NRC and GRC

May
- Trip to UK and Ireland start of month
- Two weeks in Joburg
- Two new assessment clients
- One new coaching client
- Book will be published
- Hopefully executing a chunk of client work that's the target
- No eventing

June
- Two weeks in Joburg
- Two new assessment clients
- Next board assessment?
- One new coaching client
- Eventing in SDRC
- Spend time marketing book (need to create a plan for that as soon as I get it off to the publisher)

July
- Two weeks in Joburg
- Two new assessment clients
- Next board assessment?
- One new coaching client
- Eventing in Sandringham

August
- Two weeks in Joburg
- Two new assessment clients
- Next board assessment?
- One new coaching client
- Eventing in Jo'burg? Maybe bring Filipe up to Northern Farm and work up here... a possibility?

September
- Two weeks in Joburg
- Two new assessment clients
- Next board assessment?
- One new coaching client
- Eventing in Kurland – needs some time off

October
- Two weeks in Joburg
- Two new assessment clients
- Next board assessment?
- One new coaching client
- Any chance of a trip to Dublin?

November
- Two weeks in Joburg
- Two new assessment clients
- Next board assessment?
- One new coaching client
- Any chance of a trip to Dublin?

December
- Probably one week in Joburg to finish off the year.
- One new assessment client
- Continue planning process for 2019

Figure 8: Planning the year

I'm aware that this is a bit messy and not very detailed. Everything is jumbled together. But that is my life and it comes with a degree of complexity. I'm fine with that, it works for me. You'll find a system that works for you.

Write down your objectives, print them out and keep them on your desk. I've laminated mine. The buckets and the year plan are also near to hand, because they tell me *how* I'm going to achieve my objectives. At some point I might use a SWOT analysis as described in Chapter 1, or some of the tools mentioned in Part Three.

Keep a date with yourself at the start of every month to check on your progress. If something isn't working, it's alright to change course and set a new objective or delete it, but ask yourself "Why?" Maybe you need to make it easier for yourself and build your dream in smaller steps.

Although I love technology and I use it to help me, I also use physical visual aids and I have an annual wall planner that sits above my desk and helps me to track my progress. It can look a bit intimidating at the beginning of a busy year – where is the freedom? - but it really helps me to plan and to identify roadblocks coming up. There are periods where I cannot possibly do everything I'd like to do, and that means I need to re-think or restructure things.

As you do your planning, bear in mind that different objectives will require different approaches. You might need a bit more time to figure this out. It might be worth taking a break at this point to let your subconscious tackle the issue. Put a time in your diary to come back and give it some conscious attention later. Remember, the key activities are to break the plan down into buckets and figure out the processes that need improvement.

Changing Habits

Successfully reaching your goals often means changing your habits. For example, diet and exercise objectives often need a change in lifestyle, which requires changing long-term habits and behaviours. That can be hard and you might want to get involved with support groups, both to help you cope and to entrench new values.

Putting things into buckets can help in lots of ways. You can choose your priorities and you can tackle easier tasks first or when your energy levels are low, while maintaining movement towards your objectives.

For sporting challenges break down every possible aspect of the process and put these into buckets. Looking at the buckets ask yourself - how can I make these easier or better?

Buckets might include things like diet, training hours, technique, researching new methods and approaches, finding a better coach, re-contracting with the coach you have, cross-training to make your workouts more effective, or reading books about sporting achievement, like *The Chimp Paradox* by Dr Steve Peter or *How Champions Think* by Dr Bob Rotella. Remember that small changes in multiple areas can add up to impressive performance improvements overall.

A big project might mean you invest in some apps and project tools to help you put in the hours needed to achieve your dream.

Figure out what you can do to support your objectives. There's so much information out there, particularly on the internet; it's fun to find out more about what increases your effectiveness. I've written more about changing habits in Chapter 14 - Change and Choice.

Part Three – Commitment

"Integrity is the consistency of words and actions."

Kenneth Chenault

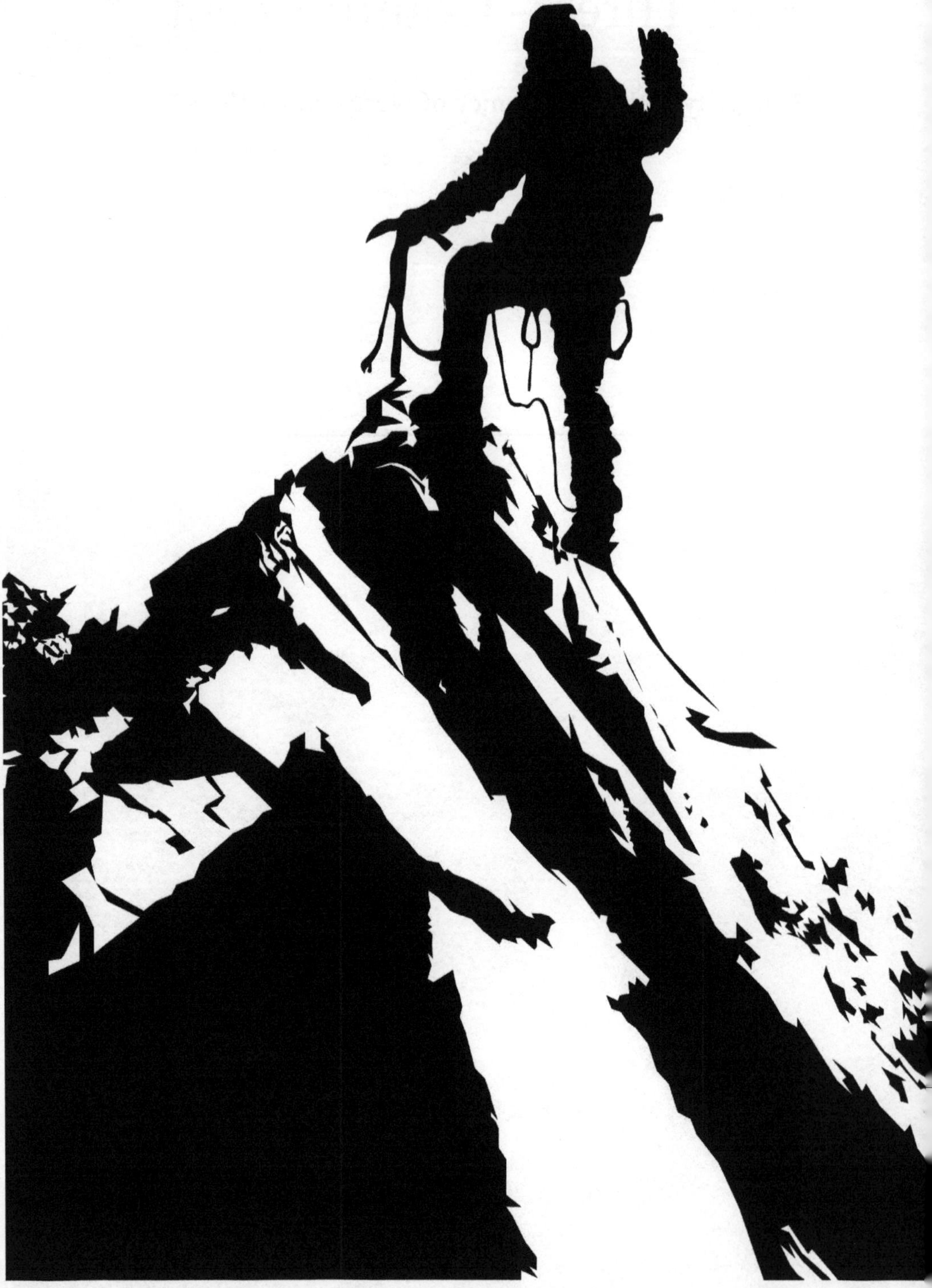

Chapter 12

Integrity

How do you define integrity? My main professional skill is assessing CEOs and other senior executives, often in the context of a CEO search process or a succession planning project. I'm often asked to assess people's integrity, but what is integrity and how do you define it? I finally came across a definition that I like in *Legacy*, James Kerr's story about the All Blacks' extraordinary run of victory in the late 2000s and early 2010s. It's very simple: integrity is doing what you say you'll do. Doesn't sound like much, does it? Many definitions of integrity are more high flying, such as this one: The quality of being honest and having strong moral principles; moral uprightness. In ethics studies, they say it's about the honesty and truthfulness or accuracy of one's actions. I like that one better, but I still prefer: Doing what you say you're going to do. Imagine a world where everyone aligned their actions and their words? Imagine a business where everyone delivered on what they said they would do? What a transformed world we would live in.

I don't think I've ever met anyone who doesn't claim, sincerely, to have integrity, but too often their words and actions don't meet up; there's a gap between our idea of ourselves and the reality of how we show up in the world. We mean well, but we don't always deliver.

Writing about integrity reminded me of a personal story that demonstrates why it matters.

I lost my mother when I was very young. Things that are connected to her are unusually important to me. One day, I was chatting to a friend of hers who told me that before I was born, she was at my mother's house and admired a picture on the wall. As she was leaving, my mother gave it to her. "That picture is in a cupboard now Sarah", she said, "I'll find it and give it to you".

For several years after that, whenever we met she would mention the picture and that she was planning to give it to me. She never did, and now I know she never will.

It was the words "I'll give it to you" that created the expectation. And with that expectation came a whole lot of feelings. Whether or not I liked the picture, I would have hung it on the wall and every time I looked at it I would have thought what a kind person my mother was, what lovely friends she had, and how much it meant that she was not forgotten.

This woman is deeply religious and was involved in politics for many years. She would certainly say of herself that she has great integrity, maybe even that integrity is one of her core values. She did not do what she repeatedly said she would do though; her actions and her values were not aligned.

The reason I've shared such a personal story about integrity is because I want to stress the real meaning we attach, both to words and actions, and how important it is that *your* words and actions are congruent, at the very least when you are making promises to yourself. In a world where US Presidential elections can be influenced by blatant lying, we may wonder whether integrity is a lost value. It's not for me to judge your choices. If you want to plan for success though, you'll need to commit to action and your actions need to reflect your commitment. Integrity is not just about doing what you've told someone else you'll do. Above all, integrity is about holding yourself to account and keeping your promises to yourself.

Take the words of Thuli Madonsela, one of the bravest women I have ever encountered. As South Africa's Public Protector she coined the phrase "state capture" to describe what was happening in South Africa under the leadership of President Jacob Zuma and his allies, the Gupta family. Madonsela has been fearless in her pursuit of justice for the citizens of South Africa and inspirational in her own right. She said: "We cannot lead others if we cannot lead ourselves. The hallmark of leadership is responsibility." This is one of the most important things we need to understand about leadership, because we must each be our own leader and shoulder that responsibility.

> For responsibility read integrity. Make the commitment to yourself and then do what you say you are going to do. This is first step in leadership.

In the next few chapters there are some tools and suggestions that should help you keep your self-leadership on track as you set out to achieve your goals. If you get stuck, you can come back to this section and see if there's an idea here that might help reset, reprioritise, or re-motivate you.

Chapter 13

Priorities

❦

Maybe it's not that you don't have a dream or an objective for the year... maybe you have too many. Some of my clients complained that they could not do the 5-Step plan because they could not decide on just three themes and then just three objectives per theme. You can have more themes of course, but if you choose three and then have three objectives per theme, that's already a lot of goals. If you manage it, you'll be very pleased with yourself. I'd challenge you to set bigger objectives, not more objectives.

Go big and focus your efforts on a few important themes rather than scattering your efforts too widely.

In my own case there are parts of my life that require ongoing management, of myself or others, but those might not appear on my list of themes. They include sport; weight; the Airbnb business; running my house, garden and social life; and the annoying management of the minor health issues that crop up as one gets older. When I set my themes I try to think about the bigger picture, and I find Step 3 in the 5-Step process helpful because the focus is on outcomes: what will make you feel great six months or a year from now? In the past two years, study – above all the pace of my research project – was a top priority. Now that's done and I'm setting bigger work objectives to fill that gap as well as concentrating on this book. My garden has been neglected and it might be a theme for next year, but this year there's a drought and I'm busy, so it will receive less attention because establishing my new business is so much more important.

Don't think that your themes have to be world beating and awe-inspiring. Some years you might choose to focus on freeing up more time to spend with your kids or to walk in the park once a week. You may want this to be the year you write a book, get the big promotion, or start a business. Or it might be the year where you devote more time to caring for an elderly relative and find a way to do it with grace and good humour. The point is to reflect on your life and spend time thinking about what you really want. If you do that, you will achieve more, and better, than you ever thought possible.

When you start the planning exercise, get some paper and a pen organised and find a quiet place where you can concentrate. When you're working on achieving your objectives throughout the year, remember the importance of focus and that we cannot multi-task; to get good results we need to concentrate.

How do you remember what to focus on as the year progresses? Keeping your priorities and objectives in mind is important, because in the everyday world we get interrupted by immediate urgencies. One of the best tools to help manage this is the Eisenhower Matrix. I first saw it in Stephen Covey's *7 Habits of Highly Effective People* in the early 1990s, and I've been recommending it ever since.

Here's how it works. A lot of our time every day is spent doing urgent tasks that come up and demand attention **now**. Technology makes it even worse. Think of the 'ping!' that announces the arrival of an email, text, WhatsApp, Tweet or even a Facebook notification. The urgent desire to see what it says and respond immediately is similar to the kick that you get from alcohol, drugs, chocolate or exercise. Your brain releases a little shot of dopamine in anticipation of pleasure.

That's not good because that means technology is addictive. You can't give up technology if you live in the real world, so the pressure of the 'ping!' adds to the stress of your everyday life. Other urgencies intrude on your world all the time, from the project that you haven't started because you were either "too busy" or procrastinating, to the sudden crisis that hits your department and means all hands on deck until it's resolved.

The Eisenhower Matrix suggests that you look at tasks in light of their importance and their urgency. We tend to enjoy doing urgent tasks because we get an adrenaline kick from them and it's satisfying to get them ticked off. That means we do the important and urgent tasks. Too often it also means that we also do tasks that are urgent, but not important. The ones that are neither urgent nor important tend to be the ones that drop to the bottom of your inbox and stay there until you eventually delete them (and that's ok, you could probably just have deleted them in the first place). The problem is that the *important but not urgent* are the ones we tend to neglect, and that's why we miss our goals.

Doing the 5-Step planning exercise is all about *important but not urgent*. The outcome – the plan for the year – is in itself an important, but often not urgent, task. That is why focussing on it at the beginning of the year can be so helpful, because we are already attuned to things like New Year's resolutions and are ready for change. It can still be hard to get stuck into thinking hard about your themes, though, and to do the work of building your goals and your plans.

Understanding the Eisenhower Matrix and the value of figuring out which tasks are important, though not urgent, and investing time and focus in those tasks, could be one of the most powerful changes you make to your life.

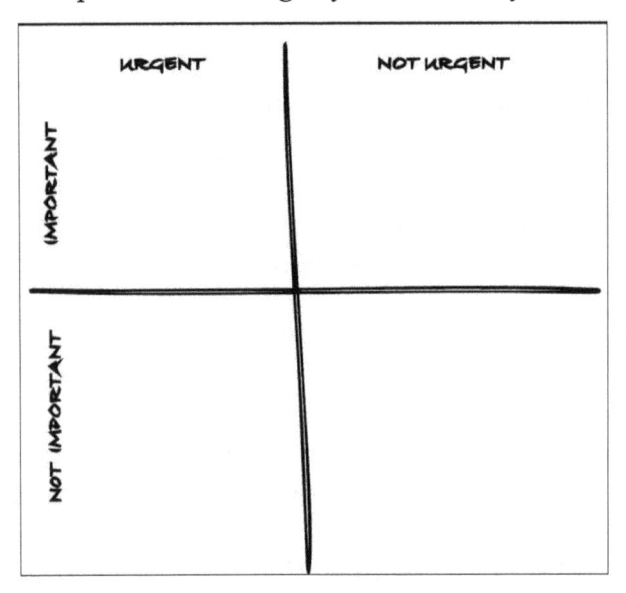

Figure 9: The Eisenhower Matrix

Whether you are sorting tasks or implementing your plan, the Eisenhower Matrix will help you to prioritise. Keep it in front of you and make sure you put your long-term objectives from the 5-Step plan into the *important not urgent* quadrant at the top right. As tasks come up, spend a moment allocating them to a box. If they are *urgent but unimportant*, think very carefully before you allocate time to them.

Chapter 13: Priorities

If they are neither important nor urgent you probably should not be doing them at all.

If they are urgent and important, meaning your house is on fire or you need to take someone to the emergency room, then you will not hesitate for a moment to prioritise that.

Here is how I use the matrix. I always have a To Do list on the go, and with a life made up of many parts, it's quite disconnected so it can be hard to prioritise properly. To illustrate the Eisenhower matrix for you, I simply took my current To Do list off my phone.

To do list
Arrange compost delivery
Sort out London trip
Call Aunt Ann
Send documents to Ireland
Book Appt with Dr D
Tidy office
Sort out paperwork
Create new shopping list template
Work on presentation for KR
Write blog article for clients
Get book endorsements
Get Peter's phone fixed
Research new 360 profiling tools
Book equine dentist
Send Christopher the Power of Small Wins
Write up coaching sessions for the week
Prepare assessment pack for next week
Learn dressage test
Pack for show

Figure 10: To Do list

Then I put every item into the appropriate box on the matrix. If saw something I could quickly sort out there and then I did so. For example, I had been talking to my stepson Christopher about *'The power of small wins'*, an article in the *Harvard Business Review* that I refer to in Chapter 1 and that I had promised to send him. Even though it was not important in the bigger picture of goals, I had promised it to him and I quickly sent it to him right away, crossing it off my to do list. That probably took less than one minute to do.

This is how I assigned the items on the matrix.

	URGENT	NOT URGENT
IMPORTANT	Arrange compost delivery Send documents to Ireland Book Appt with Dr D Work on presentation for KR Prepare assessment pack for next week Learn dressage test Pack for show Pack for Monday	Sort out London trip Call Aunt Ann Write blog article for clients Get book endorsements Research new 360 profiling tools Write up coaching sessions for the week
NOT IMPORTANT	Get Peter's phone fixed Send Christopher the Power of Small Wins	Tidy office Sort out paperwork Create new shopping list template

Figure 11: The Eisenhower Matrix filled in from my To Do list

The 'urgent and important' items needed doing that day. For example, why was compost urgent? Because in the Cape we plant in May and the soil needed to be prepared. I'm lucky to have a gardener to do that, but I needed to order the compost so that he could. Next, I was riding in a competition at the weekend and I had not learned the dressage test. That is not something I could leave until the very last minute because experience tells me my brain seems to need a couple of days to embed the sequence of movements so that I don't make a mistake on the day.

These things all needed to be actioned that day, no matter what.

The important not urgent items are the most interesting. These are more strategic or may carry deeper meaning. Many of the outcomes from the 5-Step process belong here. If you are a procrastinator you might never get to these items, yet they may be the ones that will change your life. In the case of this example, take "Write blog article for clients". I send my CEO coaching clients well researched and informative pieces that will be of interest to them. I started doing it because I realised they don't have much time to read articles on leadership, strategy and management. The topic ideas are usually triggered by something that came up in a session, so that they are pertinent and may inspire a new idea or line of thinking. This takes mental effort to do, and not being urgent, if it's not highlighted, it's something I could easily forget or procrastinate about.

Some items in this column are not urgent now but they will become urgent if I don't sort them out quickly. In this example, if I don't set up my meetings for a trip I've planned to the UK in a few weeks' time, I might lose out because the people I want to see may already be busy.

Talking about planning trips reminds me to share something I've learned over a lifetime of constant travel, which is to plan, and even pack for, my trips well in advance. Until quite recently I used to get caught up in my busy life and leave planning and packing to the last minute. Now I find I'm calmer and feel more organised if I plan several weeks in advance. If I find myself with some free time during a busy travel period I will even pack for trips that are several weeks away. This sometimes leads to a sense of adventure as I unpack, not being quite sure what's in my case. I love the feeling of getting home from a busy day or a busy week and being able to have a glass of wine, some supper and an early night because the suitcase I need for the next day is standing there waiting for me, ready to go.

If you don't pay attention to items in the *important not urgent* column, one of two things will happen: either they will suddenly become urgent and you will end up doing them in a hurry and maybe not as well as you could, or if you don't do them, they slip away, never get done, and you move further and further from achieving your goals.

When I look at the *not important, urgent* items, they belonged there because they were not important to achieving my goals, but they were important in a different way. If I've promised Peter that I will get his phone's screen fixed, then I need to do it.

Finally, the *not important, not urgent* items, like tidying my office and sorting out my paperwork. I'll get to that eventually, when I have a quiet moment. Some people are very tidy and organised about their offices. I'm not, and I've learned to live with it.

I hope that helps illustrate the point. You don't always have to lay your To Do list out in this matrix, but you should have a good sense about which quadrant in the matrix each item belongs to, and that will help you to focus and prioritise your actions.

Many of your outcomes from the 5-Step plan belong in the *important not urgent* box. You might want to develop a system where you address these tasks first thing in the morning, before you get down to anything else. It might be that, like Colette in Chapter 1, you break everything down into smaller chunks to help you identify where and how to move forward. Or you might use one of the productivity tools that I've mentioned.

Writing a big academic thesis involves months of work, and when you are in the middle of it, it can seem like an impossible task. In this case, the Eisenhower Matrix doesn't help so much because every task is important and none is urgent. Academic work is hard, and there were times when it took me three hours to write three sentences. As a believer in process, I thought - why not apply it here and see what happens? I calculated roughly the number of hours it should take to write the thesis and broke that down into a certain number of hours per month. On a spreadsheet I ticked off the hours I worked, using the Pomodoro app to make sure I recorded only the hours spent doing actual project tasks.

I did not commit to a specific number of hours per day or per week, but I made sure I met my monthly targets. Other people might have chosen to stick to a daily or a weekly target; it depends how structured your life is. Then I broke the work down into easy, harder and really hard tasks. If I did not feel full of energy I would do an easy task, such as searching for relevant articles for example, or editing my previous work. If I was full of life and raring to go I would tackle the harder tasks of writing and research.

As long as I was in my chair and working on my thesis, I would tick off the hours. I took the view that it was like climbing a Himalayan summit: if I followed the process step-by-step, I would summit the mountain at the right time. And I did.

That achievement bolstered my conviction that success is about setting objectives and then identifying the best process to achieve that success; focus on the dream outcome in the first phase, and then keep your focus on the process after that. By continually refining and improving the process, you will achieve better and better outcomes.

If you did this exercise last year and you find that your themes have not changed much, you might not see the point of setting new objectives. That's not a bad thing, but you might want to search for a fresh approach or a new process to help you implement your plan.

Take diet and weight, for example, which is a challenge for many people, myself included. Last year I said weight would be an absolute priority, and indeed, for most of the year I had it under control and was quite pleased. As the year came to an end a whole bunch of things happened that took my focus off my weight and suddenly I'm back where I started, but I don't see this as a failure.

In my case weight has been a lifelong challenge, so it's nothing new. But I do need to take another look at how I handle some aspects of my life, including travel, socialising, the odd crisis, family celebrations and so on, in order to identify a process that will help me maintain good habits even when I lose focus. Same theme, same objective, different process.

Going back to the Eisenhower Matrix, one of the problems with life is that just after you've taken some time over the New Year to create this fantastic plan, you go back to work. After the break, everything's crazy and all the super urgent things come crashing down on you demanding to be done *now!* Now you know what's important to you, how do you make sure that you get the important tasks done and stay focussed on the process of achieving your goals?

Six things can help

Here's a tool that can help you with that.

It's called the "Six things list" and it's a golden oldie. Before you go to bed each night you write a list of six things to do tomorrow. The next day you do them, before you do anything else. The six (or fewer) tasks should be listed in order of importance and every one of them should be important (see the Eisenhower Matrix above). When you're interrupted, as you will be, you compare the importance of the interruption with your six things. Unless it's more important, you continue with the six things until they're done.

Here are a few rules to help you:

Write the tasks on your list every evening, either before you leave the office or before you go to bed.

The things on the list must be important to you.

You must be able to complete each item on the list within the day. Remember, if you can't, it's too big and you need to break it down into more manageable tasks.

You complete the items on the list before you even look at the day's emails. That's quite a frightening thought, I know!

Write the list in order of importance and complete the list in that same order.

Commit to it. Do it every single day. Your productivity will soar. If you drop the habit, get back to it. It is so easy to do.

THAT FURTHER SHORE: Turn your dreams into goals and make them reality

Chapter 14

Change and choice

❧

When you jump a horse over fences you use hand-eye coordination to judge the right take-off point. Eric Winter describes it as "the shot". You can have a good shot or a bad shot. Like many things in riding horses this sounds simple, but in practice it's not easy. When you get it right it's a beautiful feeling. You and an animal that weighs about half a ton are in perfect sync, your bodies seamlessly meeting the five stages of the jump, landing and flowing forward again to the next fence. That's how it should go. When you get it wrong, as everyone, even the best professionals, do from time to time, your body tends to go into panic mode. The clear communication between you and the horse is lost and the result is either an ugly jump or a stop. If the fence is big or the pace is fast the rider quite often falls off. When it goes well the horse is like an intelligent bouncy rubber ball as he approaches the fence, and as long as that communication is kept intact and the rider has a reasonable idea of a good take off point, all she has to do is keep that connection secure and the horse can simply compress or extend his stride to reach that perfect point. When the rider is a professional, with hours and hours of training and jumping under their belt, they are usually just fine, but most riders are amateurs and don't have the time or the will to put in all those training hours. One of the challenges is that it feels much easier and safer to approach the fence slowly, but it's harder for the horse to jump the fence if he isn't powering forward.

Getting better at managing the power and jumping cleanly is all about "reps", or the 10,000 hours. The more you do, the better you get.

The purpose of this is not to give you a lesson in show jumping, but to give you some context about a fall that I had not too long ago and what I understood from it later. While I know the theory about not panicking when things go wrong, it's a lot harder when it comes to getting it right every single time in practice. My horse Filipe is a big horse. I bought him when he was young because despite his size I thought we had a rapport and felt he was incredibly talented. I was right on both counts; we have a gorgeous relationship, we have won a lot of prizes and it has been a joyous journey.

One damp Monday, our journey temporarily went from joyful to painful. I was having a jumping lesson with my coach, Daniela Smit, known as Dan. We were starting to jump bigger fences and Dan had just put the fences up to 1.20m height. Anything at this height, or over, is a significant challenge for even the best horse and rider, and the barrier can be psychological as much as physical. Despite everything I've just said, despite all my training reps and knowledge, I came around the corner without enough power, could not see the shot, flapped my legs and Filipe took a huge leap into the air, twisting his body to ensure that he cleared the fence. The problem was that three strides later there was another fence and I knew that we had no chance of clearing that. So, in mid-air I pulled on the rein to avoid the second fence. Bad mistake. He twisted some more, and I lost my balance and fell off. Ever since I broke my neck I wear an air-jacket when I jump. When you fall it deploys and inflates before you hit the ground, protecting you from neck to hip. The trouble is when you wear an air-jacket you cannot tuck and roll in the same way that you would without one. To make matters worse, my jacket malfunctioned, the only time it has done so, and did not deploy. I fell hard onto my shoulder and arm.

One of the chapters I love in *Legacy* is the one about leaving blood on the field. Wounds sustained in the field of battle are honourable wounds and most often sustained outside your comfort zone, when you stretch yourself, as we were doing that day. If it goes wrong and you get hurt, it's an honourable injury. That day I did not have much time to think about it. I was flying to Geneva that night to see a client, and I had to get myself to the airport and onto the plane. As I waited to board my upper arm was throbbing horribly, so I nipped into the ladies to get a better look. I took off my jacket and rolled up my sleeve and everything was black and blue and swelling rapidly. The woman washing her hands beside me was horrified by the sight. After we boarded I sent a text to Dan. "Not looking great." "Remember", she replied, "it's not what happens to you but how you handle it that counts".

I couldn't put my bag up into the luggage compartment, but someone kindly helped me. My arm felt strange and didn't quite work. It was very painful, so I took an anti-inflammatory, had a stiff drink followed by a sleeping pill, breaking any number of rules. Finally, I fell into a drugged sleep wondering if my arm might be fractured and what on earth I would do about that when I landed in London in the morning to catch the connection to Geneva.

Well, it was fine in the morning. Not fine exactly, the bruising and swelling took weeks to disappear, but it wasn't broken.

The reason I'm sharing this story is not to show you how tough I am, because I'm not. Rather it's to point out that because of choices I had made that day, I ended up in a position that was probably rather stupid: on an overnight flight with a potentially fractured arm. Sometimes people blame life for what happens to them and I could have blamed Dan for pushing me on a day when I was a bit stressed and off my game. Or the horse for doing something a bit silly (he did not, but riders often blame their horses for their own mistakes), or myself for agreeing to try something challenging at the wrong moment. But to be honest, the throbbing arm was simply the consequence of a series of choices I've been making all my life. Simply put, my current philosophy goes a bit like this: ride when you can; push yourself because jumping bigger fences is more challenging and ultimately more fun than jumping smaller ones; raise your game on your horse and at work; work hard at your job; never let the client down; always deliver.

Sometimes those choices are incompatible and end up meaning that where maybe I should have gone to get an x-ray, I got on the plane. The longer term consequence of that particular choice was probably a slower healing process and definitely a lot more pain, but I did the work and delivered. Luckily I had a long-sleeved shirt with me which covered the swollen dark blue bruising on my right arm when I sat in front of the client that hot June day in Geneva.

I'll never forget what Dan said. "It is not what happens to you but how you handle it that counts." It's not the first time I've faced that kind of choice and decided to do the client work. We may not have much choice about the adversities that we face in life, but we do have choices about how we handle them. Dan and I have both been through periods of real grief in our lives and we have accepted the need to respond to loss, to mourn, and to suffer. I would not judge how any person responds to tragedy. However empathetic we are, I don't believe we can put ourselves in another's shoes when they lose someone they love.

But, once the worst is over and it's time to pick up the reins of responsibility and life again, that is when the choices begin. At that point you have the opportunity to choose things that will create positive outcomes in your life. Yet how many people do you know who blame others, or events, for their situation in life, when in fact they most likely had an opportunity to choose a different path? "It's how you handle it that counts."

Think of Themba in Chapter 9. He grew up in a difficult environment where opportunities were extremely limited. He grasped every bit of luck and opportunity that came his way, consistently choosing the harder road - choosing to work and study as hard as he could. That grit defines him even now, and grit is one of the qualities that will help you to make good choices even when the road is hard.

If you want to achieve your dreams, grit will trump talent every time. In Chapter 5 I talked about how your practice needs to be deliberate, disciplined and designed to keep you focussed on the areas that need improvement. When you do the "reps", it's not just about putting the hours in, but about doing the right "reps" to take your performance to the next level.

> Exceptional people don't just do the work, they are really smart about what work they need to do.

Willpower

There are times when the choice is clear. To go to the gym, or to go home? To sit down and write the report now, or to do it at the last minute?

Sometimes you have more options than you realise. We saw that in Chapter 3, when I shared Jerome's story and explained how you can broaden your frame and create a wider range of choices. You can choose to push yourself when you run, so that every run makes you fitter, so that every run matters. Or you can stop. Or, here is a new choice, you can plod along, happy in the knowledge that any aerobic exercise, done three times a week for more than 20 minutes, leads to a longer and healthier life.

Perhaps more important than the type of choices is remembering that choice is an extraordinary gift, and something to which we should pay more attention. One of the primary benefits of planning and commitment is that we can make better, and ultimately more rewarding, choices.

If one of the important challenges you have set for this year involves change, whether at work or in your personal life, then you need to understand a bit about change and choice. As I mentioned earlier, it's important to focus on process when you are doing your planning. When you want to achieve something, big or small, you need to break it down into the tasks that will get you there and focus on accomplishing those, rather than on the finished product of the dream you want to achieve. That is often because your dream is simply too vast to think about and will put you off.

If you've never run a road race and you want to take part in a 10 kilometre event, you cannot start out by thinking about running 10 kilometres.

You start out with a plan that helps you understand what the best time of day is for you to run. How are you going to get yourself into your running shoes and out of the house on your running days? Do you need to supplement your running with other exercise like yoga or Pilates so that you increase your strength and decrease your risk of accidents? Classes might help motivate you.

Finally, you need a strategy that gets you from 0 - 10km in manageable chunks. The first day might be walking 100 steps and running 100 steps at intervals for 20 minutes. That would be a fantastic start. Focus on the steps and you build a ladder to your dream.

The same is true at work. If you decide you're going to aim for a big promotion this year, you need to understand what it will take to get that promotion and whether it's realistic in a year. The promotion is not really the aim, it's the outcome; the result.

The aim is to understand all the things you will need to do differently this year to convince your boss you're ready for a promotion. Things like showing up a bit differently at work, taking more ownership of your tasks, understanding more about the bigger picture of the business so that you can add more value in your own role.

No matter how committed you are, it's important to know that when you need willpower to make good choices, cunning planning will be involved. Our daily ration of willpower is limited. This has been researched and we now know that the attrition of willpower during a day is the result of chemical changes in the brain's executive function. Every time you make the harder choice instead of the easier choice, you burn up a little bit of willpower. In the morning, when the brain is rested and fresh, it's easy to have fruit for breakfast, go to the gym or to start your most difficult project first. Although, if you're like me and not really a morning person, it's never exactly easy to do all that, but it certainly is easier in the morning than in the evening. After a long day at work, making good work choices and saying no, for example, to the bad food choices that presented themselves along the way, you'll be tired and your executive function wants to make your choices easier. Unless you have a really good plan in place, you're going to find it much harder to resist that glass of wine or a piece of chocolate cake. Understanding this helps, because it helps you to realise that you're not a weak person - you're just a human being, like the rest of us. With a bit of planning you can make it easier to make those evening choices good ones.

Planning your choices

The 5-Step process helps you to align your choices with your true values, which is grounding and builds confidence. Putting the process and focus in place to make sure you do the "reps" will help turn your good choices into good habits by automating them.

While I was doing the research for this book I read a recent study that looked at how our social intelligence can help us make good choices. We are social beings and while we might not always make a great choice for ourselves, it's surprising how often we will do it to help someone else. If we can associate our good choices with the pride that comes from delivering benefit to others, we will make better choices. This is quite an extraordinary claim, but one that is supported by several scientific studies. Think of it this way - if you want to diet or to get fitter, and you can find a friend who wants to do the same but has less willpower than you do, you'll be more inclined to make good choices in order help them. This is one reason why groups work so well for setting and achieving objectives, not just because of the peer pressure, but because there's altruism involved, i.e. wanting to do something for the others.

> To put it simply, if you can harness your naturally altruistic inclinations to make better choices, you'll increase your chances of success.

You could add integrity to the mix: being true to yourself and your commitments, delivering every single time to the very best of your ability, not getting distracted by unimportant matters, not getting angry about things you have no control over. Instead, investing in your commitment by reading and understanding more about leadership, if you aspire to a leadership role. Exploring more about what is expected of management, if a management role is what you are after.

These goals will involve changing your habits in one way or another. If you're not in the habit of reading, you need to find time to do that. If you're not in the habit of sitting down and thinking about what the business expects you to deliver, and how you can deliver above and beyond expectations, you need to think about what must change in order for you to do that. If you get emotional or fly off the handle, or if you are not consistent in your dealings with colleagues, you need to do something about that too. If that's your challenge, I have a suggestion for you in the next chapter.

Thinking through your current habits and choices, as well as how you can better align them with your themes and your purpose, is a good way to start engaging with what you need to change.

You have a dream. You make a plan. As you set your themes and objectives, I hope that new ideas and choices emerge, and that you see your world as less binary. I know that every time I do the exercise new ideas and surprising possibilities emerge; ones I had not envisaged.

When you're ready, decide what you need to do to achieve your plan, breaking it down into the smallest chunks you can. You commit to doing it, and day by day you make the choice to stick to your plan. You have integrity. You achieve your dream.

Chapter 15

Self-management

The first time I ever saw a grown man actually screaming at someone in a meeting room was in South Africa. The place was the Spencer Stuart offices in Johannesburg, many years ago, and the man was (back then) a senior partner. I had known him for many years. We both held leadership roles in the firm and regularly met at international conventions when I was living in Paris and London. I had just moved to Johannesburg and was sitting in a staff meeting. One of the researchers, smart, opinionated, and good at her job, raised an objection to the approach the partner was suggesting. And he lost it. He simply could not bear to have his authority questioned. Sadly, it was not the last time I was to see this kind of behaviour. People who, on the surface, appear to be not only highly intelligent but also absolutely charming, yet the minute their will is crossed they go on the attack, vocally and sometimes quite aggressively.

And sadly, speaking from personal and professional experience, I would say this behaviour is more prevalent in South Africa, in work and sport, than anywhere else I've worked.

Given that my job involves assessing people from a range of backgrounds and cultures, I can report that this behaviour is not limited to any particular culture. It occurs primarily in men, or perhaps the way in which women attack is different, quieter. I've also observed bad behaviour in women leaders but it's less direct, noisy and aggressive. The purpose of this book is not to discuss South African culture, but one can imagine that this behaviour reflects some of the deep-seated insecurity that remains at the heart of the nation. Whatever the cause, it has no place in the office. When I give motivational talks and work with large groups and teams, one of my aims is firstly to highlight this issue, and secondly, to help people understand that they don't need to behave this way. That self-management is important and possible, and that we will be richer and happier as a result.

I sympathise with the problem because my own biggest development area is a tendency to become emotional and to react too quickly. I've worked on my own self-management over the years and I'm much improved, though pressure always tends to reveal one's weak spots. Consistency is one of my favourite management words and it's something I really apply to my own leadership. If you call me, no matter how I feel about the call, I will always endeavour to be pleasant, friendly and wanting to know how I can help you. That attitude seems to be a good starting point for most conversations.

Many people, even those in senior leadership roles, don't understand the concept of self-management. The concept of "authentic leadership" has not helped, because it's often misunderstood and hijacked to justify bad behaviour. If my bad behaviour is authentic, then it just means I am an authentic leader, says an executive to his coach. No, it does not, it means you are both selfish and lazy, because you have not invested the necessary time and energy to understand either leadership or authentic leadership. In fact, one of the most important aspects of leadership is self-management, because when you have yourself under control you can pay attention to others, enhancing your social intelligence and your focus. I had thought about this problem of self-management over the years, and then my brilliant dressage coach, Niall Quirk, gave me a copy of *The Chimp Paradox*.

In the book, Dr Steven Peters offers a beautiful analysis of the mind and human nature using some of the latest research as well as simple metaphors to help us understand and manage what is happening inside our heads.

He begins by describing the different parts of the brain, with simple names we can all relate to. The first is the Human. That is you, the person supposedly in charge of things, and this is the executive function of the brain. Then there's the Computer, which does all of the automatic stuff you don't have to worry about, from keeping your body working to carrying out the actions that have become automated, like Roger Federer taking a great shot in tennis. The Computer processes at lightning speed, whereas the Human processes slowly and sequentially. The third part is what Peters calls the Chimp. The Chimp is your emotional brain, technically known as the limbic brain. The Chimp is the centre of your feelings and drives the actions that emanate from those feelings. Whereas the Human is rational and thoughtful, the Chimp is insecure, emotional and impulsive. These three parts of the brain can work together in harmony, but any of them can take charge and they can all get into conflict with one another. When that happens, the Chimp usually wins.

The Human and the Chimp often do battle and that is what's happening when people behave inconsistently. I've found this metaphor to be very powerful when riding because what I do is inherently scary. I don't know anyone who doesn't get bad stage fright before they ride a cross country course. Part of the thrill is overcoming that fear, but if you let it take over, mistakes can happen. Or, if you allow yourself to obsess too much about what you have to do, you can over-process, which gets in the way of the flow, again leading to mistakes. A bit of adrenalin and stage fright is a good thing, too much can be destructive. Peters suggests that this stage fright is caused by the Chimp gradually taking over; the Chimp is irrational, emotional and tends towards catastrophic thinking, making you too scared to perform at your best. When I'm warming up at the start the Chimp is catastrophising: "What if he (the horse) forgets to jump? What if he runs away? What if I fall off? I could get hurt really badly!! What if he falls? I could get trapped underneath him! Maybe I'll lose my way on the course, that would be so embarrassing."

When you understand that, you can make friends with your Chimp. You can say to her: "Listen, it's ok, we've got this. You go and relax, enjoy the ride and we'll celebrate when it's over." I now do that if I get too wound up before I ride cross country and I can feel calm descending over me. I think about something else and don't engage in what I have to do until I'm in the starting box. There's nothing I can think about in the 20 minutes preceding that moment that will mean I have a better ride, so I box up the Chimp nicely and deliberately think about something else. When we jump out of that start box all my focus comes into play, years of training kick in, and if all goes well the ride will be the most thrilling, enjoyable five to eight minutes imaginable.

When someone loses control in a work discussion and behaves badly, one way to avoid getting into conflict with them is to remind yourself that you are not actually talking to them, but to their Chimp. That means you need to let the Chimp settle down before you try to have a rational discussion. Whatever you do, don't let your own Chimp get involved! The more you observe how your mind is operating and whether your decisions and actions are motivated by your Human or your Chimp, the more you will gain control over situations and be able to apply the ideas in this book. It takes work though, because the Chimp is strong - much stronger than the Human. Here is an example that Peters uses in the book, told in my own words.

You go for coffee with a friend and she offers you a delicious piece of cake with your coffee. You're dieting and this diet is really important to you. Unfortunately, it also means you're quite hungry. Your Chimp sees the cake and immediately says "Great, cake!" "No!" the Human replies, "I'm on a diet". (Of course this conversation is going on in your head; you haven't yet answered your friend, who is still waiting for a reply.) "But I'm hungry", says the Chimp, "and that cake looks delicious. Anyway, how can that one little piece of cake spoil anything, I've been good for ages. I deserve a reward!"

What do you think the Human is going to do? Most of us will have the cake, or at least I know I would. Peters goes on to give a lot of sound advice about managing your Chimp and becoming a better and happier person as a result.

Since it came out, *The Chimp Paradox* has been the most sold self-help book in the UK and I highly recommend it as a companion to this one, because if you really want to do something extraordinary, to achieve a really cheeky 10X target, you'll need to develop your self-management, which means you'll need to understand how your mind works and then put it to the best possible use. Extraordinary people, like the Schwarzeneggers or the Dalios of this world, seem to figure a lot of this out for themselves, but the rest of us benefit from taking ideas and advice from credible sources.

Conclusion

At this point you will either have a plan in place, or at least the makings of one, that will set you on the road to fulfilling your dreams. To achieving the unthinkable, as Pieter Engelbrecht put it when talking about leadership and responsibility. The hardest part is to deliver on the plan, but you know that already, don't you?

That is where integrity comes in.

If I was your coach we would have an initial deep conversation to discuss your values. Who are you really? What are your deepest dreams and fears? What do you really want to get out of your life? For many clients, this one session is the most important conversation they ever have.

We all had dreams when we were young, but very few people achieve those dreams. Some don't have the talent, others don't have the grit. We touched on grit only briefly in this book, but it's the thing that keeps you going, even when you feel sick, tired and miserable. Even through tragedy.

Not everyone has the talent and grit to achieve their dreams, and not everyone is prepared to put in the work that it takes either. That's why it's important to explore what you really want and to set themes that resonate with who *you* are.

You may be ambitious at work, but value even more the time spent at home with your family. You might decide you want to explore new things; maybe you want to have the simple pleasures of cooking, reading, travelling or gardening, while keeping a stable job that allows you to fund that life. You may want your job to be in an enjoyable environment where you can be happy and fulfilled and also have time to do the things you really want and enjoy.

For others, the opposite might be true. You might be a relentless overachiever who needs growth and promotion to feel rewarded and you're prepared to put the effort in. Or maybe you're an introvert and you need to put some effort into your interpersonal skills, which become increasingly important as you become more senior. Many introverts make brilliant leaders, by the way. It's not an impediment at all, you just need to work on the skills.

Use this book to help you invest the time in understanding what you want out your life, and more immediately, out of this year. Be proactive about your life's direction. Take charge of your world.

> Believe that further shore may be reachable from here.

Appendix I

Sources of information and learning.

Before going to the bookstore, I heartily recommend Ted Talks. Start with the most popular, like Simon Sinek's 'Start With Why'. Search for Ted Talks on Leadership and choose topics that interest you.

The next source of high-quality, free information is the *Harvard Business Review*. They generously give you access to three articles a month, and again, you can search for topics like leadership, HR, operations management or strategy. Even if all you do is read those three free articles per month, you'll know far more than most of your colleagues after just one year.

Senior leaders also need a view of the world. For that my favourite recommendation is *The Economist*. Although it's expensive and rather dry in tone, reading even one copy a month will give you a good grasp of global issues and trends. I'm lucky, my brother gives it to me as a Christmas present every year and I make sure to read some of every issue and lots from many issues. It's no exaggeration to say that if you read *The Economist*, you can join the conversation at any table in the world.

Books

Between work and relaxation, I read dozens of books a year. I can devour a major book in a day, though I prefer to savour them for longer. When I read lists of the '100 Best Business books' or '100 Best Books on Leadership', I generally find I've read 30—50% or more of any list. Of all these books, there are only a few that make my all-time greats list. These are the ones that I give to friends and clients as presents and that I return to again and again. At the moment, these are my top stars.

Thinking Fast And Slow by Daniel Kahneman

I love this book so much that I based my MPhil thesis on the underlying theory presented by Daniel Kahneman. His main argument is that although the field of economics is based on the premise that humans are rational decision makers, in real life we make irrational decisions and often make poor choices. He goes on to explore why we do this. Highly accessible and brilliantly written, this is the 21st century book for anyone who wants to understand how the mind works.

The Chimp Paradox by Dr Steve Peters

I've given away more copies of this book than any other. I also fully credit it, and the work of Dr Steve Peters, for helping me achieve my own childhood dream - to ride internationally under my country's flag. Steve Peters worked with Team UK cyclists in the run up to the London Olympics and they dominated the medal board with best ever results. He has taken his winning philosophy and put it into a book that can help everyone, whether in business or in sport. What I love about the book is that it's based on solid academic research but is written for the ordinary reader. If you want to achieve better results in your working life, your sporting life or both, read this one.

Legacy by James Kerr

This was the first audiobook I listened to and I realised they are a great way to increase my reading capacity. *Legacy* is the story of how the All Blacks rugby team achieved their phenomenal success from the mid-2000s onwards. They took a huge body of knowledge about leadership and sporting excellence and applied it, in detail. There's so much here - about humility, about lifelong learning, about putting your very best self on the field, and much more. I draw from it as a leader and a sportswoman and share many of Kerr's points in this book. In fact, my concept of dividing your life or your business into different buckets and then making progress in each area came from an idea in *Legacy*, where the team identified all areas of the game and then aimed to make a minimum 1% improvement in each. I do that in my own sport now, at quite a fine level of detail, and when I get it right it makes the difference between winning and losing. *Legacy* is written in a straightforward, highly enjoyable style. Of course it will resonate best if you know and love the game of rugby.

Emotional Intelligence

Social Intelligence

Focus

All by Daniel Goleman

Daniel Goleman is a seminal author when it comes to leadership. Of all his works, I particularly enjoy these three. Goleman is an academic and an original thinker, yet his style is readable and accessible.

Tools of Titans **by Tim Ferriss**

I have a love-hate relationship with Tim Ferriss because he makes me feel completely inadequate. He is a one man walking experiment, ahead of the trend on everything, but his works really are useful. Just two examples. The first is the use of virtual assistants, which he promoted in *The 4-Hour Work Week*. It took me a while to figure out how to use them, but once I did, I never looked back. You'll find my own current favourite, Hey Jude, in the section on apps.

The second comes from *Tools of Titans*, a compendium of useful information from a range of great thinkers. I've been struggling to sleep for the last few years and have not wanted to resort to sleeping pills. Ferriss recommends two tablespoons of apple cider vinegar and a tablespoon of honey, topped up with hot water in a mug and sipped as tea before bedtime. Bizarre sounding, but it works. I'm sleeping again. If I do wake up during the night I manage to get back to sleep, whereas before I would lie awake worrying for hours.

Ferriss' books are stuffed with ideas - there's probably something for everyone - and *Tools of Titans* is well worth having on your bookshelf as a reference.

Appendix II

Summary of the 5-Step process

Step 1 - Review the past year

Take a notepad and write down what you've achieved in the year. Think about things like:

- ambitions that you achieved;
- creative work;
- new skills you've developed or new behaviours you've learned;
- work successes;
- your network - people you met or got to know better;
- places you visited;
- things you achieved at home;
- your health; and
- family highlights.

Now write down any disappointments. Things like:

- setbacks at work;
- health issues;
- moments where you had to change plans or face difficulties;
- blocks or hurdles to achieving what you want;
- financial or practical challenges; and
- difficult family or friend situations.

If you did this exercise last year, now is the time to look back at last year's plan. Compare what you aimed to achieve with your actual achievements.

Next, write a headline for the last 12 months.

If you were being interviewed and asked to describe the year, what would you say? Don't be too hard on yourself – sometimes it's the journey that's important, not the goal.

Step 2 - Set your themes for this year

Steps 2 and 3 are the really fun part of this entire process and deliver the most important outcome in terms of helping you to understand where you should focus your efforts. Even if you don't see yourself as a creative person you'll find this part invigorating, because it's creative and because it's about you. First you'll set themes. These are the areas of your life that you feel need attention and change.

We're not looking at specifics here - use your reflections on the past year to help you set your themes for this year.

Write down your top three themes.

Not more than three. If you achieve them early you can add more, but for now focus on these.

Here are some suggestions to kick start your thinking process: work; business; money; leadership; skills development; work/life balance; time-management; productivity; fitness and health; family and friends; fun; travel and exploration; home; love and relationships; giving back.

Step 3 - Identify your priorities

Now you're going to brainstorm by inducing a state of "flow", which should help your creative process by reaching a deeper state of thinking about your themes. This might sound unlikely, but concentrating really hard on one thing for five minutes helps you to make interesting new connections. Don't be disappointed if it doesn't though - it might be that you need to spend more time on this later, as your plan evolves.

Take a piece of paper and a pen. Write down your first theme and, for at least five minutes (set the timer on your phone), write down ideas about how your life could be better in a year from today. Concentrate on outcomes; the best possible outcomes you can imagine. This is the time to dream.

Keep the pen moving, draw as well as write, get it all down. Don't lift the pen from the page for the whole five minutes. As you do this exercise remember to be ambitious, put no limits on what you could achieve.

Build on your ideas. If you want to be creative, what does it look like? A book, a painting course, finding a way to take your team to a new level of delivery?

Keep less glamorous objectives in mind; maybe you need to address some aspect of your health or well-being?

Try to be specific – it's not "get fit", it's run 15km a week or walk the Otter Trail. Think about outcomes; the best outcomes you can imagine. Thinking about outcomes is the clever thing about this exercise because it helps to crystallise what you really want and to put it into words. Be bold and brave at this point. Later you can refine. For now, dream of the best possible outcomes.

Now do the same for the next two themes.

You should find this process exciting and invigorating, and as you get into it, you may find that one of your priorities starts to take precedence. That is good news because it means the exercise is helping you to prioritise better.

Ideas might emerge that surprise you. This exercise can be a way of tapping into your subconscious; of pulling out those ideas you've had over the last year but forgotten as other more urgent thoughts take over. So, don't reject any surprising thoughts; they may be the important ones.

Some people have dreams that appear huge and aspirational: write a book; earn a million Rands or Dollars; start a PhD. Other people's dreams might be more practical or personal: lose weight; get fit; learn to cook really well; take your dream vacation. Does it matter? Of course not. These are *your* dreams. If you've always wanted to be a better cook, then that is your dream. Succeeding might lead to another dream, or to many happy confident hours in the kitchen. Do not allow other people to influence *your* dream; decide for yourself. If you *do* want to write a book, fantastic, this is the tool for you too.

When you've done all three, take a short break.

Step 4 – Set your goals for the year

After the break, return to your "dream sheets" and circle the ideas and objectives that appeal to you the most or that seem the most important, or both. You want to feel inspired and excited and you want these things to have a positive impact on your life.

Now write them down as a list.

Aim for about three objectives per theme – a maximum of nine. If it's a big one – like earning an important new qualification - you can focus on just that. You should end up with three to nine objectives.

Now start to break those objectives down into tasks, or create a schedule that will start you on the road to achieving them. Some of your objectives will mean changing your habits, so make sure you don't try to achieve too much at once.

Now, let's turn those plans into actions…

Step 5 - Turn your plans into actions

Take a calendar and mark up the commitments already in place.

Choose one objective from your list and write down what you must to do in January, February and March to be on track to achieve it by the end of March.

If it's going take longer, spread your actions throughout the year, but make detailed plans of your steps for the first quarter.

Write down your objectives, print them out and keep them on your desk.

Keep a date with yourself at the start of every month to check in on your progress.

References

Amabile, T.M., & Kramer, S.J. 2011. The power of small wins. *Harvard Business Review*, *89*(5), pp. 70-80.

Branson, R. 2011. *Losing my virginity how I survived, had fun, and made a fortune doing business my way.* New York: Crown Business.

Cardone, G. 2011. *The 10X rule: The only difference between success and failure.* Hoboken, NJ: John Wiley & Sons.

Clear, J. 2018. *About James Clear.* Retrieved from: http://www.jamesclear.com

Colvin, G. 2008. *Talent is overrated: what really separates world-class performers from everybody else.* London: Penguin.

Covey, S.R. 2013. *The 7 habits of highly effective people: Powerful lessons in personal change.* New York: Simon and Schuster.

Csikszentmihalyi, M. 1997. *Finding flow: The psychology of engagement with everyday life.* New York: Basic Books.

Dalio, R. 2017. *Principles: life and work.* New York: Simon and Schuster.

Emerson, D. 2011. *How good riders get good: Daily choices that lead to success in any equestrian sport.* North Pomfret, VT: Trafalgar Square Books.

Ferriss, T., Schwarzenegger, A., & Geoffroi, R. 2017. *Tools of titans: The tactics, routines, and habits of billionaires, icons, and world-class performers.* Boston: Houghton Mifflin Harcourt.

Gladwell, M. 2008. *Outliers: The story of success.* London: Hachette UK.

Goleman, D. 2006. *Emotional intelligence.* New York: Bantam.

Goleman, D. 2007. *Social intelligence: The new science of human relationships.* London: Arrow.

Goleman, D. (2013). *Focus.* New York: Harper Audio.

Goleman, D. (2015). *Focus: The hidden driver of excellence.* New York: Harper.

Harrison, K. 2018. *The 5:2 Diet and me!* Retrieved from: http://kate-harrison.com/5-2diet.

Ho, S.-Y., Tong, E.M.W., & Jia, L. 2016. Authentic and hubristic pride: Differential effects on delay of gratification. *Emotion*, *16*(8), pp. 1147-1156.

Kahneman, D. 2015. *Thinking, fast and slow.* New York: Farrar, Straus and Giroux.

Kerr, J. 2013. *Legacy: 15 lessons in leadership: What the All Blacks can teach us about the business of life.* London: Constable.

Kolb, D.A. 2015. *Experiential learning: Experience as the source of learning and development.* Upper Saddle River, NY: Pearson Education.

Lucas, B.J., & Nordgren, L.F. 2015. People underestimate the value of persistence for creative performance. *Journal of personality and social psychology, 109*(2), p. 232.

Matthews, G. 2011. *Study Backs up Strategies for Achieving Goals.* Retrieved from: http://www.dominican.edu/dominicannews/study-backs-up-strategies-for-achievinggoals.

Peters, S. 2012. *The chimp paradox: The mind management programme to help you achieve success, confidence and happiness.* London: Vermilion.

Rotella, R.J., & Cullen, R. 2015. *How champions think: In sports and in life.* New York: Simon & Schuster.

Schwarzenegger, A. 2013. *Total recall: my unbelievably true life story.* New York: Simon and Schuster.

Syed, M. (2015). *Black box thinking: Why most people never learn from their mistakes-but some do.* New York: Portfolio/Penguin.

Valdesolo, P., & DeSteno, D. 2011. Synchrony and the social tuning of compassion. *Emotion, 11*(2), p. 262.

Vohs, K.D., Baumeister, R.F., Schmeichel, B.J., Twenge, J.M., Nelson, N.M., & Tice, D.M. 2008. Making choices impairs subsequent self-control: A limited-resource account of decision making, self-regulation, and active initiative. *Journal of Personality and Social Psychology, 94*(5), pp. 883-898. DOI: 10.1037/0022-3514.94.5.883.

Lightning Source UK Ltd.
Milton Keynes UK
UKHW02f0628290618
324979UK00010B/737/P